Boston Red Sox and the Meaning of Life

Mark Rucker

MVP
BOOKS

First published in 2009 by MVP Books, an imprint of MBI Publishing Company and the Quayside Publishing Group, 400 First Avenue N, Suite 300, Minneapolis, MN 55401 USA

MVP Books are also available at discounts in bulk quantity for industrial or sales-promotional use. For details write to Special Sales Manager at Quayside Publishing, 400 First Avenue North, Suite 300, Minneapolis, MN 55401 USA.

Library of Congress Cataloging-in-Publication Data

Rucker, Mark.
    Boston Red Sox and the meaning of life / Mark Rucker.
        p. cm.
    ISBN 978-0-7603-3506-2 (plc)
    1. Boston Red Sox (Baseball team)—Anecdotes. I. Title.
    GV875.B62R83 2009
    796.357'640974461—dc22
                        2008047014

Editor: Josh Leventhal
Designer: Elly Gosso
Cover Design: Greg Nettles
Design Manager: Katie Sonmor

Printed in China

On the front cover: David Ortiz, 2007.

On the frontispiece: Red Sox logo, circa 1950s.

On the title page: Green Monster, Fenway Park.

On the back cover: Bill Lee, 1975 World Series.

Photo and Illustration Credits

We wish to acknowledge the following for providing the illustrations included in the book. Every effort has been made to locate the copyright holders for materials used, and we apologize for any oversights. Unless otherwise noted, all other images are from the publisher's collection.

AP Images: pp. 11 (Laurie Skrivan/*St. Louis Post-Dispatch*), 12 (Winslow Townson), 19 (Elise Amendola), 25 (Charles Krupa), 26 (Charles Rex Arbogast), 33 (Charles Krupa), 35 (James A. Finley), 40, 47 (Richard Drew), 113, 114, 121, 141, 142, 154 (Abe Fox), 161, 162 (Charles Krupa), 186 both (Bill Allen), 189 (Ted Sande), 199, 200, 204, 207, 209 (Harry Cabluck), 213, 215 (Paul Benoit), 217, 221, 226, 228, 238, 242, 245, 246 (Reed Saxon), 250 (Paul Benoit), 253 (Paul Benoit), 254 (Rusty Kennedy), 256 (Elise Amendola), 259 (Winslow Townson), 263 (Gerald Herbert), 265 (Ron Frehm), 266 (Winslow Townson), 269 (Winslow Townson), 270 (Jim Mone), 273 (David J. Phillip), 275 (Amy Sancetta), 276 (Winslow Townson), 279 (Winslow Townson), 280 (Nick Wass), 283 (Chris O'Meara), 284 (Charles Krupa), 287 (Michael Dwyer), 288 (Richard Vogel), 290 (Julie Jacobson), 293 (Elise Amendola), 295 (Eric Risberg), 296 (Bizuayehu Tesfaye), 300 (Chitose Suzuki), 303 (Charles Krupa), 304 (Elise Amendola), 307 (Tony Dejak), 309 (Charles Krupa), 310 (Koji Sasahara), 312 (Eric Gay), 315 (Mike Carlson), 317 (Elaine Thompson), 318 (David Zalubowski), 321 (Charles Krupa), 323 (Chitose Suzuki), 324 (Amy Sancetta), 327 (Winslow Townson), 329 (Steven Senne), 332 (Elise Amendola), 334, 342 (Charles Krupa), 352 (Steven Senne), 364 (Winslow Townson), 368, 378, 380 (Winslow Townson), 385 (Charles Krupa), 386 (Michael Dwyer), 389 (Winslow Townson), 390 (Kathy Willens), 393 (Winslow Townson), 394 (Elise Amendola), 397 (Josh Reynolds), 400 (Charles Krupa), front cover (Winslow Townson), back cover.

Boston Herald: pp. 178, 331, 338.

Boston Public Library: p. 60.

Getty Images: pp. 192 (Frank Scherschel/Time & Life Pictures), 210 (Focus on Sport), 230 (Rich Pilling/MLB Photos), 233 (Rich Pilling/MLB Photos), 235 (Gerald R. Brimacombe/Time & Life Pictures), 237 (Ron Kuntz Collection/Diamond Images), 249 (Rich Pilling/MLB Photos), 261 (Focus on Sport), 299 (Michael Zagaris/MLB Photos).

Library of Congress, Prints and Photographs Division: pp. 65, 71, 81, 101, 355.

Library of Congress, Prints and Photographs Division, George Grantham Bain Collection: pp. 43, 52, 55, 56, 69, 76, 84, 89, 91, 102, 356.

National Baseball Hall of Fame Library, Cooperstown, N.Y.: pp. 48, 63, 97, 104, 108, 118, 123, 129, 145, 153, 181, 225, 241.

New England Sports Museum: pp. 146, 363.

Shutterstock.com: pp. 2, 7, 23, 191, 351, 359, 367, 371, 372, 375, front cover background.

Transcendental Graphics/The Rucker Archive: pp. 1, 14, 16, 20, 29, 31, 36, 39, 44, 50, 66, 73, 75, 78, 83, 86, 93, 95, 98, 106, 110, 117, 125, 127, 130, 133, 134, 137, 138, 150, 157, 158, 165, 166, 169, 170, 173, 174, 177, 183, 195, 196, 203, 218, 222, 336, 341, 344, 346, 349, 360, 377, 382.

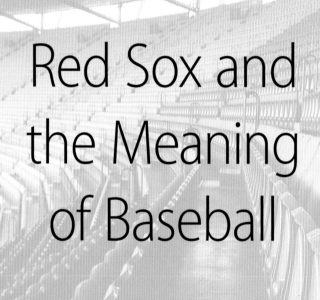

Red Sox and the Meaning of Baseball

> **"More Americans put their caring into baseball than into anything else I can think of—and most of them put at least a little of it there. Baseball can be trusted, as great art can, and bad art can't."**
>
> *William Saroyan*

Thousands of caring fans flooded into Boston's Huntington Avenue Base Ball Grounds on October 1, 1903, to catch their beloved Red Sox take on the Pittsburgh Pirates in the first-ever World Series. The crowd was eventually pushed back to the outer reaches of the outfield, where they stood for hours in the hopes of catching a glimpse of the action through the standing-room crowd. Others sat perched atop the park's outer walls, willing to put up with the discomfort for a chance to see their team battle for the baseball championship.

"Baseball is an unalloyed good. Of course, there are passions. But passion is good if it is directed toward a noble end. There's nothing bad that accrues from baseball."

Commissioner Bart Giamatti

If it's possible to be *too* passionate about baseball, the Red Sox Nation may fall into that category. Releasing the frustrations of a long 86-year drought without a World Series championship, thousands of fans spilled out into the streets of Boston following the Red Sox's victory over St. Louis in the 2007 Fall Classic. The "Curse of the Bambino" was broken, and Red Sox fans could believe once again that there is good in baseball.

> **"(Baseball) is the best of all games for me. It frequently escapes from the pattern of sport and assumes the form of a virile ballet. . . . The movement is natural and unrehearsed and controlled only by the unexpected flight of the ball."**
>
> *Jimmy Cannon*

Baseball can indeed be like a ballet, as this game of inches produces subtle and lightning-fast reactions, such as an infielder leaping over a careening base runner. Keystone combos who work together for years are able to perfect their balletic moves with harmony and grace, while fulfilling the goal of all this kinesthesis: getting the runners out. In September 2007, rookie second baseman Dustin Pedroia soars gracefully above a sliding Toronto base runner to complete a double play.

> "To compare baseball with other team games is to say the Hope Diamond is a nice chunk of carbon. The endless variety of physical and mental skills demanded by baseball is both uncomparable and incomparable."

Bill Veeck

Boston third baseman Harry Lord is high in the air to receive a throw as Cleveland's Elmer Flick has just dashed underneath to reach the base. The physical and mental skills required to make this play are betrayed by the grace of the leaping Lord's midair pose. He had to calculate the timing and height of his jump, get his body and glove in position for the incoming throw, and remain aware of the runner charging in from second base—all at the same time and all without time to reconsider or adjust.

"Ninety feet between bases is perhaps as close as man ever comes to perfection."

Red Smith

This photograph helps to illustrate why 90 feet is the perfect distance between the bases. As Washington's Roy Sievers charges full-tilt down the line, Red Sox catcher Sammy White throws toward a stretching Pete Runnels at first base. Over the years, as athletes have gotten bigger, faster, and stronger, and equipment has been refined and perfected, the 90-foot distance remains the great equalizer, helping to prevent high-scoring games while still giving the batter a chance to reach first safely on a squibber. The "bang-bang" play at first base remains a staple of the game.

> "It's played by people, real people, not freaks. Basketball is played by giants. Football is played by corn-fed hulks. The normal-sized man plays baseball and the fellow in the stands can relate to that."
>
> *Bill Veeck*

David Ortiz and Dustin Pedroia are not freaks by any measure, but the six-foot-four, 230-pound Ortiz and the five-foot-nine, 180-pound Pedroia illustrate that baseball players indeed come in all shapes and sizes. Pedroia makes the most of his size by stealing bases, scoring runs, and swooping up ground balls, while Ortiz uses his bulk to blast home runs over the fences. Together, the two have helped the Red Sox become a dominant team in baseball.

"Players in baseball are like the links in a chain, the chain being no stronger than its weakest link. They perform their actions not so much in unison as serially."

Michael Novak, in The Joy of Sports

There was no weak link in Boston's double-play combination of 1946. Here second baseman Bobby Doerr (in midair) has just rifled a throw to Rudy York at first base to complete the double play after receiving the toss from shortstop Johnny Pesky (right). The Red Sox turned 163 double plays that season while committing fewer errors than any other team. The chain was strengthened by a dangerous lineup anchored by Ted Williams, which led the majors in hits and runs scored en route to securing the team's first pennant in nearly three decades.

"Baseball is continuous, like nothing else among American things, an endless game of repeated summers, joining the long generations of all the fathers and all the sons."

Donald Hall, in Fathers Playing Catch with Sons

Since 1912, generation after generation of fathers and sons has been coming to Fenway Park to watch their beloved Red Sox. While the sport of baseball has a continuity and repetition to it, every game brings a new and different set of circumstances that makes the outcome wholly unpredictable. When you have a good seat in the ballpark, you can view the whole field in motion and observe the chain of events that determines each moment. The devoted fans will come out early to take in the pregame preparations, hoping to glean some new insight or simply to spend a little more time with their heroes.

"You can learn little from victory. You can learn everything from defeat."

Christy Mathewson

It is hard to imagine that David Ortiz and the rest of the Red Sox felt like they had learned much after losing to the Yankees in heartbreaking fashion during the 2003 American League Championship Series. After taking a 4–0 lead in the deciding seventh game at Yankee Stadium, it all unraveled for Boston in 11 innings. But the lessons were learned, and the team bounced back the very next year. Mounting an unprecedented comeback to defeat the Yankees in the 2004 ALCS after falling behind three games to one, the Red Sox went on to win the world championship, ending 86 years of learning about defeat.

> **"It's easy to have faith in yourself and have discipline when you're a winner, when you're number one. What you got to have is faith and discipline when you're not a winner."**
>
> *Vince Lombardi*

Faith has rarely been in short supply among the players and fans that have been a part of the Red Sox family, even through decade after decade of not being a winner. For the 2004 Red Sox team—the members of which playfully referred to themselves as the "Idiots"—discipline may not have been the dominant characteristic, but the talent, faith, and free-wheeling attitude was the perfect recipe for success. Pedro Martinez was the epitome of that combination.

> "Every day is a new opportunity. You can build on yesterday's success or put its failures behind and start over again. That's the way life is, with a new game every day, and that's the way baseball is."
>
> *Bob Feller*

Pitching coach Sal Maglie (second from left) is demonstrating something to pitchers Robert Carlson, Don Schwall, and Darrell Massey during spring training in 1961. The players are experiencing that feeling of a fresh start that comes about with every spring training. These three rookie pitchers, not long out of high school, were enjoying their first taste of spring training, hoping for a new opportunity. Schwall found it, finishing with a 15–7 record in his debut season. Carlson and Massey, however, never pitched in a major league game.

"It's spring fever. That is what the name of it is. And when you've got it, you want it. Oh, you don't quite know what it is you *do* want, but it just fairly makes your heart ache, you want it so!"

Mark Twain

The Boston ballplayers at Hot Springs, Arkansas, in March 1902 have spring fever, and they know what they want: They want to win. The team had finished in second place in the inaugural season of the American League in 1901, and the veteran Cy Young (second from right) is ready to evaluate the rookies, tryouts, or walk-ons with whom he is posing. Another interested observer is Ed "'Nuf Ced" McGreevy (peering over Young's right shoulder), Boston's uber-fan and owner of the Third Base Saloon—the last place you stop on your way home.

> ## "The true harbinger of spring is not crocuses or swallows returning to Capistrano, but the sound of the bat on the ball."
>
> *Bill Veeck*

Jason Varitek isn't looking for swallows but rather is admiring the flight of the ball soaring through the Florida air during spring training in 2008. While ballplayers of previous eras often had to take on winter jobs to supplement their baseball incomes, that is not true for today's stars. But even if they are able to use the offseason to work with personal trainers and maintain their workout regimes, many players arrive at camp a little out of shape. These preseason sessions give the players a chance to get back in shape and relocate their baseball timing.

"It's the fans that need spring training. You gotta get 'em interested. Wake 'em up and let 'em know that their season is coming, the good times are gonna roll."

Harry Caray

These fans at a Red Sox–Orioles game during spring training in 2006 are ready to let the good times roll, more than two weeks before the start of the regular season. The Red Sox have been spending their spring training at City of Palms Park in Fort Myers, Florida, every year since 1993, after nearly 30 years at Winter Haven and as many as 15 different sites before that, dating back to 1901. Wherever the spring training locale, the Red Sox are always warmly welcomed at the sunny retreats.

> ## "If we had no winter, the spring would not be so pleasant. If we did not sometimes taste of adversity, prosperity would not be so welcome."
>
> *Anne Bradstreet*

The Boston players posing here at Hot Springs for spring training in 1909 tasted enough adversity and were ready for some prosperity, after posting three straight losing seasons from 1906 to 1908. As an added incentive, Ed McGreevy (in front, wearing a "Boston" shirt) promised a diamond ring to the Red Sox player who stole the most bases in the upcoming season. The team, meanwhile, was economizing all the way, with some players wearing jerseys that date back to 1902.

"Baseball is really two sports: the Summer Game and the Autumn Game. One is the leisurely pastime of our national mythology. The other is not so gentle."

Tom Boswell, in How Life Imitates the World Series

There was a lot of money and prestige riding on this critical game of the 1915 World Series, with the Philadelphia Phillies back against a three-games-to-one wall. So, it must have been just a bit more frustrating than usual for Philadelphia's Dode Paskert to be thrown out at second base by Boston catcher Pinch Thomas. You can almost hear the batter telling the home plate umpire Bill Klem, in so many words, that his colleague making the call at second base needs medical attention for his eyes.

> **"I cannot agree with critics who claim there is too much stress put on the little leagues. To me, that is so much hokum. Boys must have the spirit of competition in some way, and there is none better than baseball."**
>
> *Joe Cronin*

Young Mike Yastrzemski, just four years old, doesn't appear to be feeling the stress of pitching in his dad's home ballpark during a father-son game in 1966. While the elder Yaz began his career at the ripe age of 21, the younger Yastrzemski never rode the spirit of competition to the big league level. Many other major leaguers have spawned professional ballplayers, among them former Red Sox slugger Tony Armas, former Red Sox catcher Tony Pena, and longtime outfielder Tito Francona, whose son Terry, of course, led the Red Sox to two world championships as manager.

> **"I believe in the Rip Van Winkle theory: that a man from 1910 must be able to wake up after being asleep for seventy years, walk into a ballpark and understand baseball perfectly."**
>
> *Commissioner Bowie Kuhn*

While the Red Sox have been playing in the same ballpark for nearly a century, a time traveler from 1912 (Fenway Park's first season) who woke up in 2009 would surely have some questions—like, "What's that big green wall in left field?" But Bowie Kuhn's point is well taken, as the fundamental rules of the game have changed little. The pitcher still tries to get his pitch by the batter, the batter still tries to reach base safely, and the fielders still try to stop him from doing so.

BOSTON AMERICAN LEAGUE BASE BALL COMPANY

RED SOX

Mr. Harry Stovey

133

NOT TRANSFERABLE

Robert Quinn

PRESIDENT

> "The one constant through all the years has been baseball. America has rolled by like an army of steamrollers. It's been erased like a blackboard, rebuilt, and erased again. But baseball has marked the time. This field, this game, is a part of our past. It reminds us of all that once was good, and what could be again."

W. P. Kinsella, in Shoeless Joe

Harry Stovey, whose fabulous baseball career many believe warrant his inclusion in the Hall of Fame, saw baseball go through several major changes, on the field and off. He retired from the game after the 1893 season but stuck with it as an observer through the decades, long enough to hold this 1930 season pass to Fenway Park. It may be safe to say that Stovey kept up with the national pastime and, knowing what once was good, was watching ballgames from the nineteenth century well into the twentieth.

> "Take me out to the ball game,
> Take me out with the crowd.
> Buy me some peanuts
> and cracker jack,
> I don't care if I never get back."

Jack Norworth

Carl Yastrzemski is enjoying more than peanuts and cracker jack in the clubhouse after a game. The sausage, potato salad, and cold beer is the perfect meal after defeating the New York Yankees in a key game in September 1978. Yaz and the rest of the Red Sox Nation would lose its collective appetite, however, after losing to New York in a one-game playoff on October 2 to determine the American League Eastern Division crown.

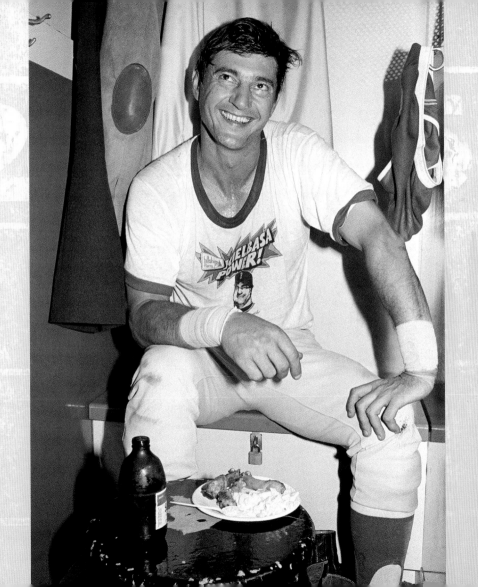

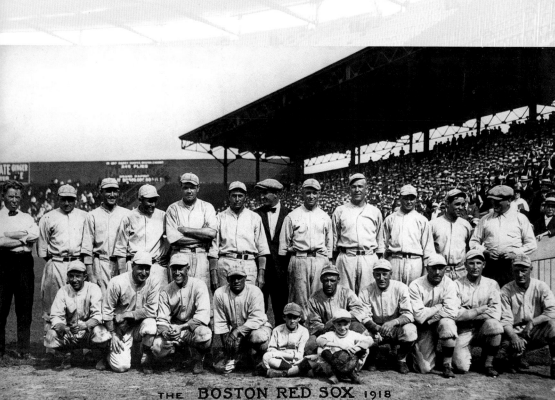

THE BOSTON RED SOX 1918

LAWLER MILLER JONES THOMAS RUTH HOOPER MAYS SHEAN KINNEY STRUNK McINNIS BARROW

SCOTT DUBUC BUSH WHITEMAN SCHANG MAYER WAGNER AGNEW COFFEY

MASCOT & BATBOY

Baseball Royalty: The Red Sox of the Early Twentieth Century

"We have a ball team in this town that's known both near and far.
Ev'ry man that's in the team has proved himself a star.
With Speaker out in center field, and Joe Wood standing in the box,
There's not a team in either league can equal the Red Sox."

Verse one of "The Red Sox Speed Boys,"
Henry E. Casey and Martin Barrett

Although "The Red Sox Speed Boys" may lack musical merit, it is a wonderful celebration of the Red Sox dynasty of the 1910s. In 1912, the collection of players toasted in musical form by Martin Barrett and Henry E. Casey won 105 games en route to a world championship. It was the team's first of what would be four championships in the decade.

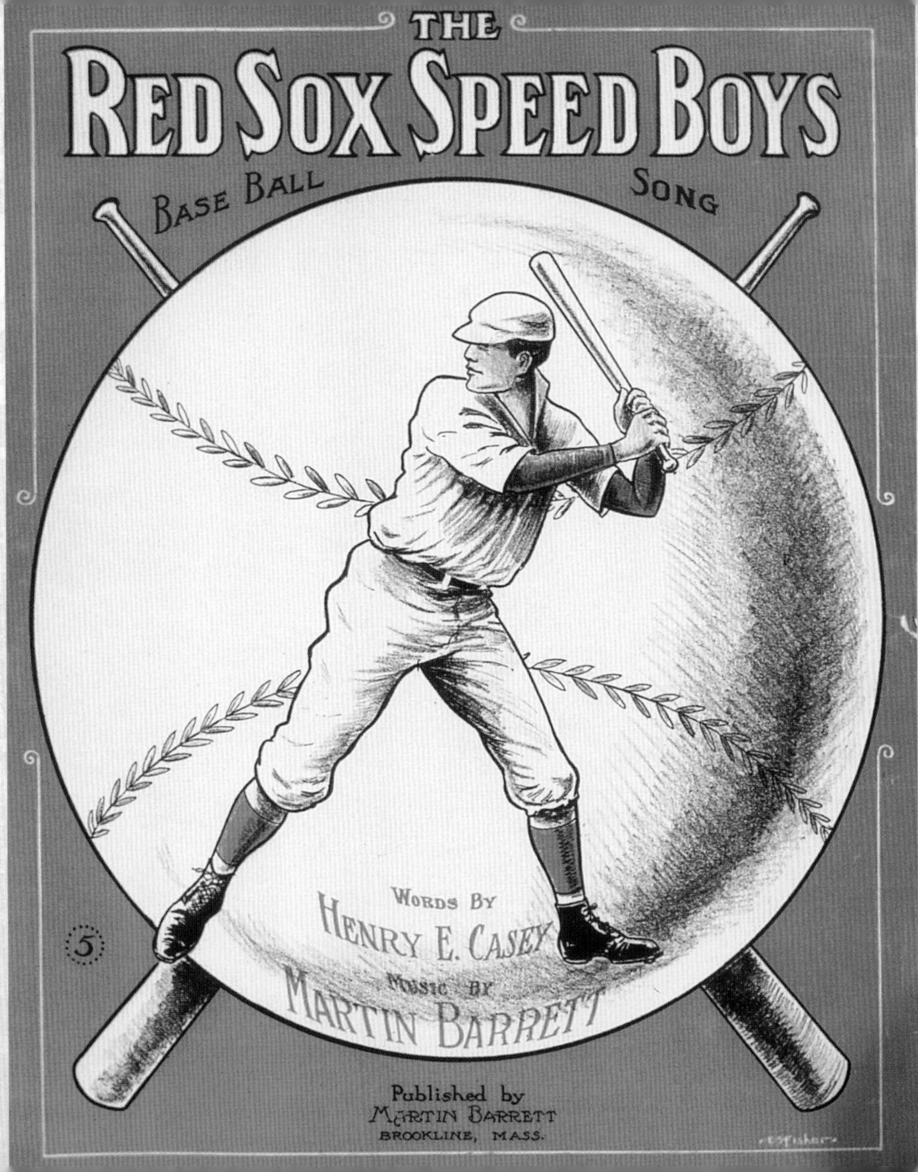
THE
RED SOX SPEED BOYS
BASE BALL SONG
WORDS BY
HENRY E. CASEY
MUSIC BY
MARTIN BARRETT
5
Published by
MARTIN BARRETT
BROOKLINE, MASS.

"We have a bunch of pitchers that are right there with the ball, Ray Collins, Bedient, Buck O'Brien, Larry Pape, and Hall. For catcher we have Cady and for second base have Ball, And for first base we have Clyde Engle, who can take the place of Stahl."

Verse two of "The Red Sox Speed Boys,"
Henry E. Casey and Martin Barrett

Buck O'Brien (left)—seen here sparring with Bill "Rough" Carrigan during spring training in 1912—was one of the pitchers "with the ball" that season. He went 20–13 in 1912, his second year in the majors. He played his final major league game in August 1913 and retired with a 29–25 lifetime record. Carrigan, who shared catching duties with Hick Cady, was with the team from 1906 through 1916 and played on three World Series winners.

"Let's all up and root for the Red Sox Speed Boys. They like the noise. We like the plays that's made by Speaker, Joe Wood, Hooper, Lewis, Wagner, Yerkes, Gardner, and Stahl. Bill Carrigan how he can catch the ball."

Verse three of "The Red Sox Speed Boys,"
Henry E. Casey and Martin Barrett

Duffy Lewis, Larry Gardner, Tris Speaker, and Heinie Wagner were mainstays for the so-called Speed Boys in 1912. Wagner and Gardner manned the left side of the outfield, while Lewis and Speaker roamed left and center fields, respectively. All four played for the 1915 champion team as well, although Wagner had to miss much of the season and all of the postseason with injuries.

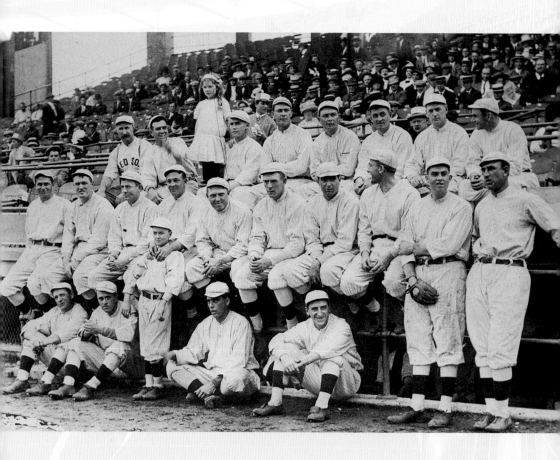

"They are the pennant winners,
that's plain to see.
Champs they will be. Take it from me,
That when the world series is played,
They'll put the nationals in the shade.
Let's root for the Red Sox now!"

Verse four of "The Red Sox Speed Boys,"
Henry E. Casey and Martin Barrett

The Red Sox indeed cruised to the pennant in 1912, holding first place continuously through the final three and a half months of the season. They went on to defeat the formidable New York Giants of John McGraw and Christy Mathewson in a true October classic. Four of the World Series games were decided by one run, and Game Two ended in a tie after 11 innings.

> **"It's hard to believe now, after so many decades of frustration, but from 1912 to 1918 the Boston Red Sox were the best team in baseball. . . . Even more importantly: When they made it to the World Series, they won every time."**

Joseph Wallace, in World Series:
An Opinionated Chronicle

Joseph Wallace wrote his book about the history of the World Series in 2003, the eighty-fifth season without a World Series win for the Red Sox and their fans. In the sixteen seasons from 1903 to 1918, Boston had a perfect 5–0 record in the Fall Classic (and they were denied a chance to make it 6–0 when the National League's New York Giants refused to participate in the 1904 event). Over the next eight and a half decades, the Red Sox won four American League pennants but lost every one, and every one in seven games.

CHAMPIONS 1912
RED SOX
WORLD'S SERIES
FENWAY PARK · BOSTON ·
Souvenir Biography and Score Book ·

Price, 10 Cents

"We won from the most important clubs in America and we are entitled to the honor of champions of the United States. There is nothing in the constitution or playing rules that requires its victorious club to submit its championship honors to a contest with a victorious club in the minor league."

John T. Brush, president of the New York Giants

Jimmy Collins and the Red Sox raised a gigantic "Worlds Champions" banner over their ballpark in 1904. The champion club from the upstart American League had the temerity to defeat the National League's Pittsburgh Pirates in the first World Series the previous October. This outcome rankled many members of the National League, who considered themselves the last word in baseball, as evidenced by John Brush's comment following the 1904 season. Alas, there was no postseason contest held that year, but a backlash against Brush and the National League brought about the return of the Fall Classic in 1905.

> **"As the players came from the clubhouse for practice, an uncouth figure that brought a titter from the stands shambled along behind them. His jersey shirt stretched across his missive body like a drumhead, and his arms dangled through its sleeves. . . . The great (Cap) Anson saw (Cy) Young. 'Is that the phenom?' he asked with a sneer."**

The Sporting Life *magazine*

Cy Young, who began his career in the big leagues with the Cleveland Spiders in 1890, may not have looked like a professional athlete at first glance. His big, round, and disheveled appearance did not impress Cap Anson, who had built dominating teams in Chicago during the 1880s. But appearances can be deceiving, and it did not take long for Anson to change his tune. Young soon emerged as one of the game's all-time great hurlers.

"Y is for Young,
The magnificent Cy.
People batted against him,
But I never knew why."

Ogden Nash

Even a poet was moved to write about Cy Young. Ogden Nash, who was only nine years old when the larger-than-life pitching star hung up his cleats for good, included Young in his poetic "ABC of Baseball Immortals," known as *Line-Up for Yesterday*. Along with other Red Sox stars of yore Babe Ruth, Tris Speaker, and Jimmie Foxx (the "X" entry), Young, the winningest pitcher in baseball history, was rightly honored with the "Y" entry in Nash's alphabet.

"Too many pitchers, that's all, there are just too many pitchers—ten or twelve on a team. Don't see how any of them get enough work. Four starting pitchers and one relief man ought to be enough. Pitch 'em every three days, and you'd find they'd get control and good, strong arms."

Cy Young

In Cy Young's day, pitchers were expected to pitch every three days and usually all nine innings of the game. During his eight seasons in Boston, Young averaged more than 34 complete games and 340 innings per year, with a peak of 384 innings in 1902. By comparison, nobody on the 2007 world champion Red Sox pitched more than 205 innings that season, and nobody had more than one complete game. Over his 22-year career, Young pitched more innings than anybody in baseball history, and he holds another all-time record that will *never* be broken: 511 wins.

> # "When I was a rookie, Cy Young used to hit me flies to sharpen my abilities to judge in advance the direction and distance of an outfield-hit ball."

Tris Speaker

From the time he was a 19-year-old rookie with Boston in 1907 until his final season with the Philadelphia Athletics at the age of 40, Tris Speaker was always working on sharpening his baseball skills, and it paid off with a Hall of Fame legacy. Shown here during his MVP season in 1912, Speaker's .345 career batting average ranks sixth all-time in major league history; his mark while a member of the Red Sox was .342. He was also known for his speed on the bases and exquisite glove work in the outfield.

"Any man who can look handsome in a dirty baseball suit is an Adonis. There is something about the baggy pants, the Micawber-shaped collar, and skull-fitting cap, and the foot or so of tan, or blue, or pink undershirt sleeve sticking out at the arms that just naturally kills a man's best points."

Edna Ferber, from Bush League Hero

From this photo, it might be hard to characterize Boston outfielders Duffy Lewis, Tris Speaker, and Harry Hooper as Adonises, but the baggy uniforms and other style points didn't stop this trio from becoming baseball's best outfield trio in the early part of the twentieth century. From 1910 through 1915, Lewis manned left field, Speaker roamed center, and Hooper covered right field as the team racked up wins and pennants. Lewis is the only one of the three not enshrined in Cooperstown.

"The American boy starts swinging the bat about as soon as he can lift one."

Tris Speaker

Tris Speaker's image swinging a bat was captured on baseball cards, tobacco premiums, toy pennants, lapel buttons, and sporting goods guides. Here his image was used to promote the Wright & Ditson sporting goods company in 1913 in an effort to compete with industry giants Spalding (which produced the official baseballs and guides for the National League) and Reach (which did the same for the American League). The experiment was short-lived, as Wright & Ditson were crushed within a few years beneath the weight of Spalding's and Reach's powerful distribution networks.

Wright & Ditson
GUIDE TO
BASE
BALL

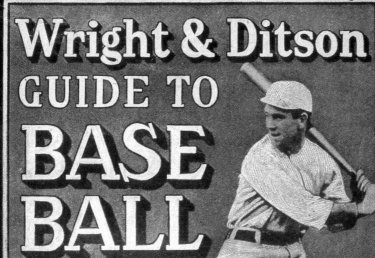

PUBLISHED BY
Wright & Ditson

> ### "With a swoop like that of a chicken hawk, (Jimmy) Collins would gather up the bunt and throw it accurately to whomever should receive it. The beauty about him was that he could throw from any angle, any position on the ground or in the air."

John B. Foster, in Spalding's Official Baseball Guide for 1902

Third base was home for Jimmy Collins. He offered dexterity, quickness, great leaping ability, an accurate throwing arm, and resourcefulness. In a game against the New York Highlanders in the early 1900s, Wee Willie Keeler laid down one of his classic bunts. Keeler was used to reaching first without even a throw, but Collins pounced on the dribbler, grabbed the ball with his bare hand, and shot it to first baseman Candy LaChance in one motion to get Keeler by a step. No one had seen this move before, and soon it was being attempted throughout the league.

"Can I throw harder than Joe Wood? Listen, my friend, there's no man alive can throw harder than Smoky Joe Wood!"

Walter Johnson

Most baseball fans know the name Walter Johnson—winner of 417 career games and one of the first five players inducted into the Baseball Hall of Fame. Joe Wood posted only 117 career victories, and he didn't win any past the age of 25, when injuries short-circuited his career. But for a few seasons, Wood was dominant. Known as "Smoky Joe" for his blazing fastball, Wood went 34–5 with a 1.91 ERA in 1912. Reminded of the great Johnson's statement many years later, the humble Wood said, "Oh, I don't think there was ever anybody faster than Walter."

JOE
WOOD
BOSTON
A.M.

OUT

> ## "Wherever I was, I played baseball. That's all I lived for. When I sat up on the front seat of that covered wagon next to my father, I was wearing a baseball glove. That showed anybody who was interested where I wanted to go."
>
> *Joe Wood*

The nation's obsession with the game of baseball dates back to the 1860s, and almost as long is the obsession with collecting mementos of a favorite ballplayer. Joe Wood was obsessed with playing the game, as opposed to observing. While Wood carried his glove everywhere with him, boys across the country would carry their tobacco cards or game cards to demonstrate their loyalties. This card is part of the "Tom Barker Baseball Card Game" and was one of the units in a parlor game for fans.

"I don't know anyone who ever went through life without making a mistake. Everybody who has ever lived has committed sins of their own. I've tried to make up for it by living as clean a life as I could. I'm proud of the way I've lived, and I think my family is, too."

Ed Cicotte, in 1965

Ed Cicotte is best known for his part in throwing the 1919 World Series as a member of the notorious Chicago Black Sox. Prior to that, he stayed out of trouble as a pitcher for Boston from 1908 to 1912. In 1909, he went 13–5 with a 1.97 ERA and helped out in a relief role as needed. The tobacco card shown here was issued by Sweet Caporal cigarettes in 1911, a time when Cicotte was not facing the torments revealed in the quotation from him more than half a century later.

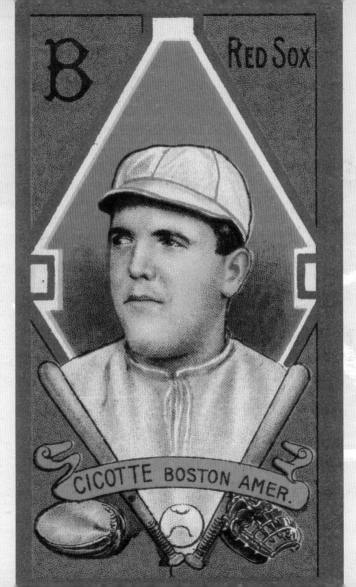

B

RED SOX

CICOTTE BOSTON AMER.

81

"It was held by many of our Base Ball critics—those who write of the game and players—that the series lacks spirit and determination; that the losers seemed to be as well satisfied to lose as to win, because the financial returns were quite alike; that there was in evidence . . . a purely commercial atmosphere and not one of the sport."

John B. Foster, in Spalding's Official Base Ball Guide for 1916

The photo of Boston outfielder Duffy Lewis sliding hard into third base during Game Three of the 1916 World Series suggests some element of spirit and determination—although the third base coach does seem to be distracted by something apparently more interesting off toward left field. The financial returns for the winning Red Sox players after the series was $3,910, while the losers from Brooklyn each took home $2,835, not insignificant sums for the poorly paid professional baseball player of the 1910s.

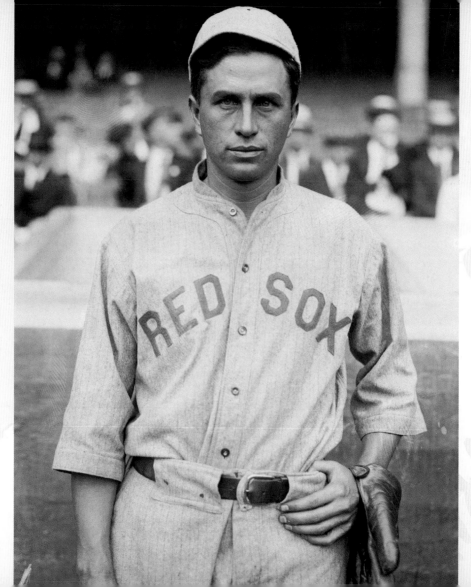

"It has been the experience of World Series that the games have brought to the fore at least one player whose work throughout was most sensational. It seems as if the honor of being the greatest individual success in 1916 belongs to (Harry) Hooper of the Boston club."

Spalding's Official Baseball Guide for 1917

Red Sox supporters long admired the play of Harry Hooper, not least of all during Boston's four World Series appearances of the 1910s. During the 1912 series, Hooper collected nine hits and made a game-saving catch to rob New York's Larry Doyle of a home run. He batted .350 and hit two home runs in the 1915 series, and the following October, he chipped in with six runs and a .333 average over the five games.

86

"HOOP" (HARRY) HOOPER
Left Fielder, Boston Americans
Supplement to Boston Sunday Herald, July 18, 1909
See Story on Sporting Page

"Harry Hooper had everything. He could hit, he could field, and he could throw. I never saw a man who could go back on a ball as well as Harry."

Babe Ruth, in Babe Ruth's Own Book of Baseball

Harry Hooper fielded his way into the Hall of Fame and into the hearts of teammates and fans during his 12 seasons as right fielder for the Red Sox (1909–1920). Babe Ruth, Hooper's teammate from 1915 to 1919, described how Hooper was not only expert at chasing down deep flies hit over his head, but could also charge in on the ball for a shoestring catch as well as anybody, including Hooper's legendary outfield mate, center fielder Tris Speaker.

"A smart, shrewd ball player, always working for the best interests of his club, and an inspiration to his fellow players."

The Sporting News, *on Larry Gardner*

Brought up from the minors as a general-interest infielder in 1908, Larry Gardner was Boston's full-time starting third baseman by 1912, a position he held until the end of his career. Gardner, seen here in 1912, was an essential cog in the Red Sox machine that won the World Series in 1915 and 1916 but was sent to Philadelphia after the 1917 season in exchange for first baseman Stuffy McInnis. Today the speedy Gardner ranks among the top five on the Red Sox franchise list for career triples, stolen bases, and sacrifice hits.

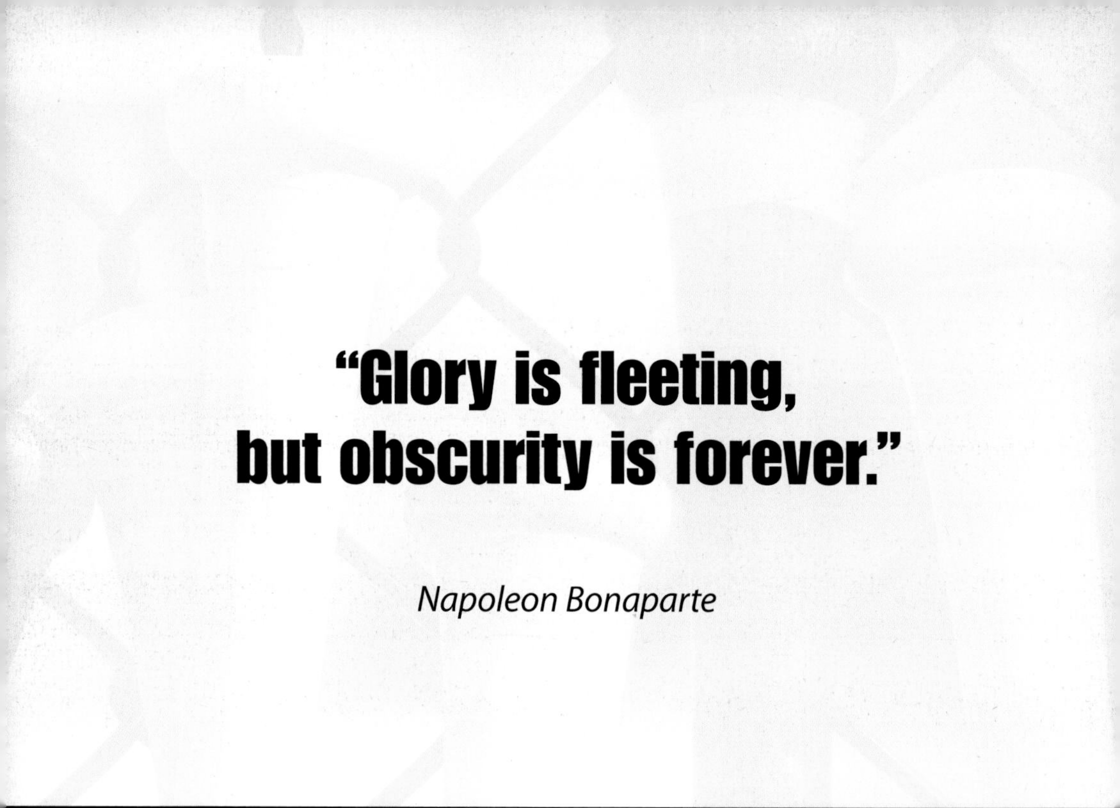

"Glory is fleeting, but obscurity is forever."

Napoleon Bonaparte

Larry Gardner enjoyed plenty of glory in his day, but he wallows in relative obscurity today. A top-quality infielder for 17 major league seasons (9 with the Red Sox), Gardner and his achievements are little remembered in the twenty-first century, but there is no doubt that Boston's Royal Rooters of the time appreciated his talents and effort. He is pictured here (far right) with other once-glorious but now-obscure Boston teammates—Dick Hoblitzell, Everett Scott, and Jack Barry—in 1916.

> "Aim at perfection in everything, though in most things it is unattainable. However, they who aim at it, and persevere, will come much nearer to it than those whose laziness and despondency make them give it up as unattainable."
>
> *Lord Chesterfield*

Ernie Shore (right, shown with infielder Hal Janvrin in 1915) attained near-perfection on June 23, 1917, in a game against the Washington Senators. After Boston's starter, Babe Ruth, was ejected for disputing a walk to the game's leadoff batter, Ray Morgan, the right-handed Shore came in to take over. Morgan was promptly thrown out trying to steal second base, and Shore went on to retire the next 26 batters. The no-hit, no-walk, no-error performance by Shore is not technically considered a perfect game, since the game's first batter reached base, even though it wasn't by Shore's hand.

93

"**There was a day when (Joe) Bush could get by on sheer speed. Those were the years he picked up the nickname of 'Bullet Joe.' Nowadays, however, Bush couples speed with his fork ball and a few, a very few, judiciously placed curves.**"

F. C. Lane

"Bullet" Joe Bush played for Boston from 1918 to 1921 before being shipped to the Yankees. His fastball was still working while he was with the Red Sox, and in 1918 he won 15 games and posted a 2.11 ERA. After missing the entire 1919 season, he won 15 games again in 1920 and went 16–9 in 1921. Although he was an effective pitcher for Boston, it surely rankled Sox fans to watch him rack up the finest winning percentage in the league (26–7, .788) for the Yankees in 1922.

"Pitching a game is really a memory test, like playing a game of cards where you must remember every card that has been played."

Howard Ehmke

Sidearmer Howard Ehmke passed the memory test with flying colors during his first season with the Red Sox in 1923, when he won 20 games. He followed with a 19-win campaign in 1924 before slumping to a 9–20 record in 1925—while posting a respectable 3.73 ERA on a team that won only 47 games. After starting the 1926 season with a 3–10 mark, Ehmke was traded to Philadelphia in mid-June. Ehmke always made sure that the hitters remembered him, too, as he led the league in hit batsmen six times between 1920 and 1927.

"Forty is the old age of youth; fifty the youth of old age."

Victor Hugo

At age 40, Jack Quinn still looked and acted youthful, leading the Red Sox with a 3.27 ERA. He pitched his final game on July 7, 1933, six days after his fiftieth birthday—in the youth of old age, by Victor Hugo's count. Quinn's tenure with Boston (1922–1925) was a relatively small piece of his 23-year major league career. Such longevity allowed Quinn to get his name in the record books under several entries, including oldest player to collect an RBI (49), oldest pitcher to win a major league game (49), and oldest pitcher to start or finish a World Series game (47).

The Babe, Before the Curse

> "You know, I saw it all happen, from the beginning to the end. But sometimes I still can't believe what I saw, this 19-year-old kid, crude, poorly educated, only lightly brushed by the social veneer we call civilization, gradually transformed into the idol of American youth and the symbol of baseball the world over."

Harry Hooper, on Babe Ruth

Harry Hooper and others watched with a combination of incredulousness and awe as this young phenom from Baltimore, wide-eyed and green as a field of weeds, burst on the scene in 1914. Babe Ruth's incredible talent and limited life experience combined to produce wild achievements, both on and off the field— some of which might have ended his career in today's world of media scrutiny and the big business of Major League Baseball. Ruth (far left) is photographed with teammates Ernie Shore, Rube Foster, and Del Gainer early in his career.

104

"As soon as I got out there, I felt a strange relationship with the pitcher's mound. It was as if I'd been born out there. Pitching just felt like the most natural thing in the world. Striking out batters was easy."

Babe Ruth

Babe Ruth was born to play baseball, there is no doubt about it. That a person's genetic make up could be fully realized by playing a specific sport, available in only certain places on the globe and at only certain times in history, makes one wonder about things such as destiny and fate. Was Ruth preordained to play baseball? Was it a coincidence that he was born in the land where this unusual game was devised? We should all be so fortunate to have found our calling and excel at it, as George Herman Ruth did.

"In most big league ball games, there comes an inning on which hangs victory or defeat. Certain intellectual fans call it the crisis; college professors, interested in the sport, have named it the psychological moment; big league managers mention it as the 'break,' and pitchers speak of the 'pinch.'"

Christy Mathewson, in Pitching in a Pinch

In Babe Ruth's first World Series start——Game Two of the 1916 series at Fenway Park——the "pinch" came in the opening stanza. After giving up an inside-the-park home run to Brooklyn's Hy Meyers (seen in this action photograph) with two outs in the first inning, Ruth proceeded to pitch 13 scoreless innings, before Boston won the game, 2–1, in the bottom of the fourteenth. For the young pitcher, it was the beginning of a record streak of $29\frac{2}{3}$ scoreless innings in World Series play (which he extended during the 1918 series).

> ## "Ruth made a grave mistake when he gave up pitching. Working once a week he might have lasted a long time and become a great star."
>
> *Tris Speaker, on Babe Ruth*

While hindsight may make Tris Speaker sound like a fool, this statement reflected a popular sentiment of the time. Babe Ruth had been a dominating pitcher for four solid seasons in Boston, and some believe that Ruth might have been a 300-game winner had he remained a mounds-man. But the kid could hit, too, and as a pitcher, he took the field only once every four days, whereas in the outfield he could contribute in all 154 games. In 1918, the Red Sox played him in the outfield on off days from pitching, but production suffered. In 1919, he played 111 games in the outfield while starting just 15 from the mound. In 1920, he was sold to the New York Yankees—and the rest is history.

SPRING & SUMMER
CATALOG
1920

"BABE" RUTH
THE HOME RUN KING
USES EXCLUSIVELY
THE LUCKY DOG
GOODS

D&M
SPORTING -GOODS-

MADE BY
The Draper-Maynard Co.
PLYMOUTH, N.H.U.S.A.

FOR SALE BY

FISHER'S BOOK STORE

Somerset, Pa.

110

"I won't be happy until we have every boy in America between the ages of six and sixteen wearing a glove and swinging a bat."

Babe Ruth

Most people think of Babe Ruth in a Yankee uniform: hitting home runs in a Yankee uniform, playing the outfield in a Yankee uniform, and promoting products in a Yankee uniform. But, as this Draper and Maynard sporting goods catalog illustrates, the Babe was selling sports-related products to boys on a national basis as a pitcher, and in a Red Sox uniform, before he wound up in New York. This advertisement, though dated 1920, depicts Ruth wearing a Boston road uniform from 1918, in one of his earliest appearances in an advertisement.

> # "A man loved by more people and with an intensity of feeling that perhaps has never been equaled before or since."

Harry Hooper, on Babe Ruth

More than just a dominating baseball player, Babe Ruth was a cultural icon, a multimedia star in an era of limited media. He appeared in movies and advertisements, hawking everything from candy and cigarettes to underwear and motor oil. After moving to New York, the attention and bright lights surrounding Ruth only intensified. His popularity even extended across the globe, as evidenced by the enthusiastic greeting he received on a visit to Japan in November 1935.

> ## "You gotta be a man to play baseball for a living, but you gotta have a lot of little boy in you too."
>
> *Roy Campanella*

Players like Babe Ruth never ceased being kids. The Babe even seemed to like being around kids better than he did adults. His visits to hospitals, orphanages, and schools were not publicity stunts cooked up by his agent, but were places that Ruth truly wanted to be, and he continued to pursue these activities long after his playing days were over. In December 1941, he visited with young patients at the Hospital for Joint Diseases in New York.

"He ruined one of the American League's great ball clubs by systematically selling star after star to the rich owners of the Yankees."

Babe Ruth, on Harry Frazee

Harry Frazee, owner of the Red Sox from 1916 to 1923, was the most hated man in Boston. He made a habit of using his ballclub as a means to finance his other operations, mainly his stage productions. This led him to sell the greatest baseball star of all time to the Yankees for a sum of $100,000—though not specifically to fund the musical *No, No, Nanette*, as is popularly believed. In addition to Babe Ruth, Frazee also sent to New York over the years: catcher Wally Schang, shortstop Everett Scott, outfielder Duffy Lewis, and pitchers Joe Bush, Waite Hoyt, Carl Mays, and Herb Pennock.

H.H. FRAZEE
presents

THE ROUND-THE-WORLD TRIUMPH

The MOST
SENSATIONAL
MUSICAL
SUCCESS
of this
GENERATION

"No, No,
Nanette"

Book by
FRANK MANDEL
& Otto Harbach

Music by
VINCENT YOUMANS

Lyrics by
Otto Harbach
& Irving Caesar

> **"You know, for me, this is just like an anniversary myself, because 25 years ago I pitched my first baseball game in Boston for the Boston Red Sox. . . . It's a pleasure for me to come up here and be picked also in the Hall of Fame."**
>
> *Babe Ruth, in his Hall of Fame induction speech, 1939*

When Babe Ruth first took the mound in Boston in 1914, there was no Hall of Fame, but by the time the first class of Hall of Famers was announced in 1936, Ruth's name was one of five on the list, along with Ty Cobb, Walter Johnson, Christy Mathewson, and Honus Wagner. Ruth was a unique and supremely talented individual, and it was clear from nearly the beginning that Ruth would forever be placed among the eternal heroes of baseball, both in the public consciousness and in a dedicated museum.

Lefty, Double X, and the Boston Doldrums

Al Schacht (center) at spring training with Herb Pennock (left) and Heinie Manush, 1936

"All things considered, Grove is the best lefthander that ever walked on a pitcher's slab. He surpasses everybody I have ever seen. He has more speed than any other lefthander in the game."

Connie Mack

Lefty Grove lived his life quietly and played the game of baseball with efficiency and consistency. He pitched for Connie Mack's Philadelphia Athletics from 1925 to 1933, racking up nearly 200 wins. The Red Sox took advantage of one of Mack's all-star sell-offs in 1934 and acquired the dominating southpaw in exchange for two mediocre players and $125,000 in cash. Although Grove's best years were behind him, he won 20 games for Boston in 1935 and led the league in ERA four times during his time in a Red Sox uniform (1934–1941).

"Lefty Grove could throw a lamb chop past a wolf."

Arthur Baer

Lefty Grove had a mean fastball, all right—and he could also entice many eager young boys to sit down with a bowl of Wheaties for breakfast. As the dominating pitcher of his era, Grove was an attractive subject for advertisements and promotional ventures nationwide. In this ad, which appeared in 1937, Grove is joined by fellow baseball Hall of Famers Joe DiMaggio, Mel Ott, Jimmie Foxx, Bob Feller, and Carl Hubbell, as well as golfer Tony Manero, tennis star Ellsworth Vines, and swimmers Lenore Kight Wingard and Jane Fauntz.

"A tart temper never mellows with age, and a sharp tongue is the only edged tool that grows keener with constant use."

Washington Irving

Tales of Lefty Grove's temper are renowned among baseball historians. As a member of Connie Mack's Philadelphia A's, Grove was fast, wild, and full of fury. Mack said that when Grove played in Philly, he was a thrower, and after being traded to Boston, he became a pitcher. Seen here sitting with manager Joe Cronin, Grove is even smiling. He never had jaw-dropping success in Boston that he enjoyed in Pennsylvania, but he may have had a happier time.

"When Neil Armstrong first set foot on the moon, he and all the space scientists were puzzled by an unidentifiable white object. I knew immediately what it was. That was a home run ball hit off me in 1933 by Jimmie Foxx."

Lefty Gomez

According to contemporary accounts, nobody hit the ball harder than Jimmie Foxx. In 1936, "Double X" arrived in Boston (part of Connie Mack's clearance sale in Philadelphia) and immediately made himself at home by hitting 41 home runs and driving in 143 runs. Two years later he reached the astonishing RBI total of 175 to go along with 50 homers and .349 average, earning him the American League Most Valuable Player Award.

"A low-ball hitter and a high-ball drinker."

Anonymous Red Sox teammate, on Jimmie Foxx

Baseball fans may wonder how it is that Jimmie Foxx, at age 33, became the youngest player to reach 500 career home runs (a record since broken), yet went on to hit only 34 more after that. One teammate's assessment of Foxx tells the story. Foxx was a hard liver, and that was hard on his liver, then hard on his swing, and then hard on his career. Perhaps the most surprising thing is that Foxx, his baseball career, and his alcoholism were able to thrive for so long and so productively.

"Doldrums. 1.a. Ocean regions near the equator characterized by calms or light winds. b. The calms characteristic of these areas. 2. A period of inactivity, listlessness, or depression."

American Heritage Dictionary of the English Language

When infielder Marty McManus was handed the managerial reins in mid-June 1932, the Red Sox were not literally at sea, but they surely were in the doldrums. Not only had the club not won a pennant since 1918, it hadn't had a single winning season. Boston finished dead last eight times in the ten seasons prior to 1932. McManus, shown here holding the lineup card for the day's game, couldn't do much to get the team back on course. The Sox lost 11 of the first 12 games under McManus and ended the season in last place once again.

"The odds were against us, but we deserve to be where we are."

Steven Gerrard, star soccer player for Liverpool

After finishing in sixth place in 1931, Boston hoped to improve its odds by bolstering the lineup with the acquisition of Dale Alexander from Detroit and Smead Jolley from the Chicago White Sox early in the 1932 season. Although Alexander posted a .372 average in his 101 games with Boston and Jolley led the squad with 18 homers and 99 RBI, the Red Sox managed their worst season in franchise history, with a record of 43–111 (.279) and 64 games out of first place. Pictured here are Jolley, Rabbit Warstler, and Alexander, who with the rest of their teammates deserved to be where they were: dead last.

"I was walking down the street wearing glasses when the prescription ran out."

Comedian Steven Wright

We can be sure that Danny MacFayden, right-handed hurler for the Red Sox from 1926 to 1932, was called "four eyes" and other epithets countless times. He was not the only bespectacled major leaguer, active or retired, but wearing glasses always attracted attention on the diamond. Despite his visual enhancements, MacFayden had a respectable 17-year career, during which he won 132 games. He posed with his glasses for this 1933 Goudey bubble gum card.

DANNY MACFAYDEN

BIG LEAGUE CHEWING GUM

137

"Wes & Rick Ferrell"

> **"My father used to play with my brother and me in the yard. Mother would come out and say, 'You're tearing up the grass.' Dad would reply, 'We're not raising grass. We're raising boys.'"**
>
> *Harmon Killebrew*

Father Ferrell was raising boys too, and the two Ferrell boys surely tore up the grass in their North Carolina yard as youths. Pitcher Wes and catcher Rick, a Hall of Famer, played together on the Red Sox beginning in 1934, until the two were traded to the Washington Senators in midseason in 1937. During their time in Boston, Rick was a .300 hitter and Wes was a two-time 20-game winner, leading the league with 25 wins in 1935. The pitcher-catcher brother duo was featured on a Goudey baseball premium card in 1936.

"The best baseball legs I ever saw, including Cobb."

Paul Krichell, baseball scout, on Bill Werber

Posed here with Joe Cronin in 1936, Bill Werber isn't showing his remarkable legs, but he does enjoy a laugh with his manager after ending his contract holdout. A third baseman on the baseball field, Werber was also an All-American basketball player at Duke University, and a speedster indoors and out. In 1934 and 1935, Werber out-stole everyone else in the American League, with 40 and 29 stolen bases, respectively. He also batted .321, collected 200 hits, and scored 129 runs (all career highs) in 1934, his first full season with the Red Sox.

> **"Brevity being the soul of wit, no memorable baseball quotation comes close to matching the verbal economy, elegance, and exactitude of Mike Gonzalez's classic scouting report of the 1920s that described a young Moe Berg as 'Good field, no hit.'"**
>
> *George Vass*

Moe Berg had a 15-year major league career, the last five (1935–1939) as a backup catcher with the Red Sox. He was a lifetime .243 hitter who hit only six homers in more than 1,800 career at bats. But his baseball statistics are not the most interesting part of Berg's life story. In 1943, the Ivy League-educated athlete was recruited by the Office of Strategic Services (OSS), which later became the CIA, to be a spy for the U.S. government during World War II. The eccentric Berg was described by Casey Stengel as the "strangest man ever to play baseball."

"As the game goes on, I not only like it for what it is, but I get to thinking of other games and other players, and I like that, too. Bobby Doerr goes back of second to rob Charlie Keller of a single to center, and I remember other great keystone sackers I have seen, Eddie Collins and (Charlie) Gehringer and (Rogers) Hornsby, and so on around the diamond, and through the day."

John K. Hutchens

Fans who have sat in ballparks watching baseball for years might find that, despite the sport's continuity, every game, every play on the diamond is in some way unique. The fine work of second basemen of generations past was both mirrored and transformed by the artistry of Bobby Doerr, seen here turning a double play over a hard-sliding Chicago base runner. A career Red Sox, Doerr was named the starting second baseman for the American League all-star team five times, and he ranks among the Red Sox franchise leaders in most statistical categories.

"He's better than his brother Joe, Dom-i-nic Di-Mag-gio."

Popular song sung by Red Sox fans

Well, he was *not* better than his brother, but Dom DiMaggio was an excellent outfielder for the Red Sox for 11 seasons and a seven-time all-star. Nearly three years Joe's junior and about five inches shorter, Dom also was not the great looker that Joe was. He didn't marry Marilyn Monroe or any other movie star. He wasn't known as "Joltin' Dom" or the heartthrob of the nation, but he did have one little ditty sung for him, and only Boston fans would sing it. The words may have been incorrect, but the sentiment was genuine.

> ## "You know, sometimes, when they say you're ahead of your time, it's just a polite way of saying you have a real bad sense of timing."
>
> *George McGovern*

Jim Tabor had a dream rookie season for the Red Sox in 1939. He hit .289, had 14 home runs and 95 runs batted in, and played full-time at third base. Unfortunately for him, Ted Williams also showed up in Boston that year, concealing the accomplishments of all his teammates. Tabor did persevere, though, and remained a steady infielder for the Sox until 1944, putting up solid numbers every year. But it was Tabor's bad timing that kept him out of the headlines and in the shadow of a baseball giant who shared the field with him.

149

"An unfulfilled vocation drains the color from a man's entire existence."

Honore de Balzac

Cecil "Tex" Hughson's unfulfilled career didn't drain his existence, but it did deny him a place among the all-time greats. Owning a fastball to match most any in the game, Hughson burst on the scene in 1942, winning 22 games in his first full season with Boston. Fighting the sophomore jinx, he won just 12 games in 1943 but bounced back the following year with 18 victories. After losing one season to military service, the Texan returned in 1946 and won 20 games. With a star career seemingly ahead of him, Hughson developed difficulties with his pitching arm, and by 1949 he was done.

> ## "One who gains strength by overcoming obstacles possesses the only strength which can overcome adversity."
>
> *Albert Schweitzer*

Joe Dobson had a tough time growing up during the Depression as one of 14 children. He also had the added disadvantage of losing a thumb and part of a finger on his left hand from an explosives accident as a child. The right-handed Dobson was still able to hold a glove and pitch effectively despite the injury and he was a mainstay on the Red Sox staff from 1941 to 1950. Dobson compiled a 106–72 record with Boston, with his best season coming in 1947, when he posted 18 wins and a 2.95 ERA.

153

> **"Asthma doesn't seem to bother me anymore unless I'm around cigars or dogs. The thing that would bother me most would be a dog smoking a cigar."**

Comedian Steve Allen

Dave "Boo" Ferriss probably wouldn't find much humor in Steve Allen's remark. Ferriss, who suffered from chronic asthma, persevered to post a 21–10 record and 2.96 ERA for the Red Sox in his rookie season of 1945. He improved to 25–6 in 1946 and earned a complete-game, shutout victory in Game Three of the World Series. It was not long, however, before asthma proved his downfall. His breathing disorder combined with an increasingly sore arm pushed Ferriss out of the rotation by 1948, and he was out of baseball in 1950 at the age of 28.

"York is part Indian and part first baseman."

Detroit sportswriter, on Rudy York

Rudy York overcame early prejudices against his Native American heritage to become one of the stars of the American League in the 1930s and 1940s. After an impressive first nine seasons with the Detroit Tigers—with whom, as a rookie in 1937, he set records for most home runs (18) and RBI (49) in one month—York was traded to Boston before the 1946 season. His timing could not have been better, as the team reached the World Series for the first time in 28 years. York drove in 119 runs in what would be his only full season as a Red Sox.

"A major league baseball team is a collection of 25 youngish men, who have made the major leagues and discovered that, in spite of it, life remains distressingly short of ideal. A bad knee still throbs before a rainstorm. Too much beer still makes for a unpleasant fullness. Girls still insist on tiresome preliminaries. And now there is a wife who gets headaches or a baby who has colic."

Roger Kahn

This collection of veterans and youngsters reached the ideal of a league pennant in 1946. Numerous players on the squad had recently returned from military service in World War II, most notably Ted Williams (top row, far right), Johnny Pesky (front row, second from left), and Dom DiMaggio (front row, third from right). To be sure, Williams, Pesky, DiMaggio, and the rest of the Red Sox had personal problems that plagued them during the season, but manager Joe Cronin (front row, sixth from left) finally had a winner in Boston.

"You don't just accidentally show up in the World Series."

Derek Jeter

Neither team in the 1946 World Series showed up by accident. The St. Louis Cardinals were making their fourth trip to the Fall Classic of the decade, and Boston posted the franchise's best record since 1912 to capture the pennant by a comfortable 12-game lead over Detroit. But once they got to the series, the trouble began for the Red Sox. Outgunned by the championship-tested Cardinals, the Sox were trounced in Game Four at Fenway Park by a score of 12–3, as St. Louis accumulated 20 hits. Ted Williams, who batted .200 in the seven-game series, could only stand in disbelief.

AMERICAN LEAGUE
1 2 3 4 5 6 7 8 9 H
ST. LOUIS 0 3 3 0 1 0 1 0 4 20
BOSTON 0 0 0 1 0 0 0 2 8

"I thought the pole was plenty. . . . When something like this happens, it makes you feel pretty good. But I don't want to die just yet."

Johnny Pesky, at Old Timers' Day

Having the foul pole at Fenway Park named after him was no doubt a big honor for Johnny Pesky, even if it was a little strange to be memorialized while he was still alive. In September 2007, he was on hand to celebrate his eighty-seventh birthday, and he is seen here enjoying a piece of cake in front of the pole named in his honor.

> **"You have two hemispheres in your brain, a left side and a right side. The left side controls the right side of your body, and the right controls the left half. It's a fact. Therefore, left-handers are the only people in their right minds."**
>
> *Bill Lee*

Lefty Mel Parnell spent his entire 10-year career with the Red Sox and won 123 games, more than any southpaw in franchise history. Lefties are a rare and valuable commodity in baseball, but—with Fenway's short left field enticing right-handed batters to loft balls over the Green Monster—few lefties have established star credentials while pitching in Boston. The eccentric Bill Lee was a lefty, too, and he won 94 games in his 10 seasons as a Red Sox—although many would question whether he was in his right mind.

"Promise, large promise, is the soul of an advertisement."

Samuel Johnson

The promise of a career like George Kell's was used to sell breakfast cereal to kids in the mid 1950s. A future Hall of Famer, Kell spent only one full season with the Red Sox, but his all-star play and popularity earned him a contract with Wheaties. Kell was a journeyman, going from team to team to fill holes in major league lineups, as he did with the Red Sox between June 1952 and May 1954.

"Probably the best thing that happened to me was going nuts. Nobody knew who I was until that happened."

Jimmy Piersall

Jimmy Piersall was well known among baseball fans, particularly in Boston, during his six seasons as a starter for the Red Sox (1953–1958), but he received his widest national attention following the release of the film *Fear Strikes Out* in 1957, starring Anthony Perkins and based on Piersall's autobiography, which chronicled Piersall's battle with bipolar disorder. Overcoming his demons, Piersall played in the majors on and off for 17 seasons and was an all-star in 1954 and 1956.

"Spread the diaper in the position of the diamond with you at bat. Then fold second base down to home and set the baby on the pitcher's mound. Put first base and third together, bring up home plate, and pin the three together. Of course, in case of rain, you gotta call the game and start all over again."

Jimmy Piersall, on how to change a diaper

Jimmy Piersall was a good father. This photograph had not seen print since it was taken in the 1960s, and when the image surfaced on eBay, Piersall's daughters requested copies of the photo so they could show it to their kids. One generation passes to the next its care, concern, and intelligence, in sport and in family life.

> **"A good catcher is the quarterback, the carburetor, the lead dog, the pulse taker, the traffic cop, and sometimes a lot of unprintable things, but no team gets very far without one."**
>
> *Miller Huggins*

From 1951 to 1959, Sammy White was the Red Sox's designated quarterback and traffic cop. His offensive production was respectable if not spectacular (he batted .264 during his time in Boston), but he was an integral part of the team for nearly a decade, calling pitches and handling the pitching staff. He played more games at catcher than any Red Sox backstops besides Jason Varitek and Carlton Fisk before finishing his career with the Braves and Phillies.

173

"He's on the team, boys. He's on the team because he's going to put money in all our pockets. And remember this, boys. He's only the first. There's more coming, and they're hungry."

Leo Durocher

Though Leo Durocher is talking to his Brooklyn Dodgers about Jackie Robinson, the same words might have been spoken to the Boston Red Sox before Pumpsie Green joined the team. Green made his debut with the Red Sox in July 1959, 12 years after Robinson entered the league. The Red Sox were the last major league team to integrate, and Pumpsie Green was no Jackie Robinson, but Green permanently etched his place in franchise history by being the first African-American to don a Red Sox uniform.

"High temperatures mean low air molecule densities. Low air molecule densities mean low air molecule weight per cubic foot. Consequently, high temperature cities have low air molecule densities. Low temperatures mean high air molecule densities. High air molecule densities mean high air molecule weight per cubic foot. Consequently, low temperature cities have high air molecule densities."

Mike Marshall, baseball pitcher and Ph.D.

Chances are that Vic Wertz (left) and Frank Malzone were not speaking of the weather in these terms in Scottsdate, Arizona, on March 10, 1960. With Wertz cooling off with an ice cream bar, and teammate Malzone placing an icepack on his head, the pair were at spring training when the temperature soared to a not so staggering 80 degrees. The outfielder and the infielder were likely putting on a show for a local photographer on a slow news day.

"Poets are like baseball pitchers. Both have their moments. The intervals are the tough things."

Robert Frost

Pitcher Earl Wilson had plenty of tough intervals during his baseball career. Signed by the Red Sox in 1953, Wilson was the first African-American ballplayer signed by the team, although military service kept him off the roster until 1959. He made his big league debut exactly one week after Pumpsie Green became the first black player to take the field for Boston, and Wilson spent the next several seasons bouncing between the majors and minors. His big moment came on June 26, 1962, when he threw a no-hitter against the Los Angeles Angels. Celebrating with Wilson after the game are catcher John Tillman and Dick Radatz.

"The pitcher is happiest with his arm idle. He prefers to dawdle in the present, knowing that as soon as he gets on the mound and starts his windup, he delivers himself to the uncertainty of the future."

George Plimpton

It's hard to imagine that big Dick Radatz was happiest when idle, considering he appeared in 270 games for the Red Sox over his first four major league seasons. The 6-foot-6, 230-pound Radatz used his imposing size and lively fastball to save 100 games and win 49 for Boston from 1962 to 1965. The uncertainty that George Plimpton describes began for Radatz when he left Boston for Cleveland, where his speed was diminished, and dawdling may have become the more attractive option. He won only three more games in the final three seasons of his short career.

181

"I'm not getting paid to field. I'm getting paid to hit."

Dick Stuart

Hard-hitting Dick Stuart was most comfortable in the batter's box, as exhibited by the 42 home runs and 118 RBI he produced for the Red Sox in 1963. He spent just two seasons in Boston (1963 and 1964) and led the American League in errors by a first baseman in both. Stuart was made to be a designated hitter but, sadly for him, was born in the wrong part of the century.

"I knew when my career was over. In 1965, my baseball card came out with no picture."

Bob Uecker

In 1965, a baseball card came out with pictures of four Red Sox rookies. Bill Schlesinger's career was basically over before it started, as he made one plate appearance in 1965 and never played in another major league game. Jerry Moses fared slightly better, spending nine seasons as a reserve catcher with seven different teams, while Mike Ryan was a part-time backstop with the Sox, Phillies, and Pirates from 1964 to 1974. The star of Boston's rookie class in 1965 was clearly pitcher Jim Lonborg, whose 15-year career included a Cy Young Award season for Boston in 1967.

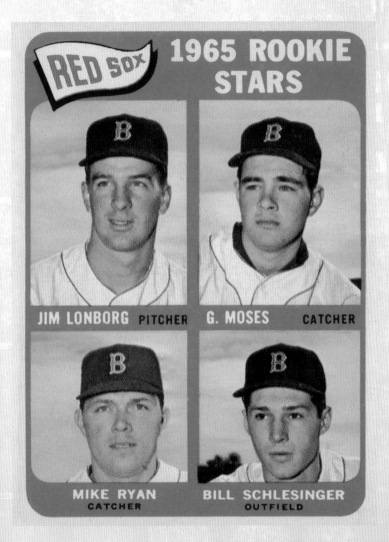

RED SOX 1965 ROOKIE STARS

JIM LONBORG PITCHER   G. MOSES CATCHER

MIKE RYAN CATCHER   BILL SCHLESINGER OUTFIELD

185

186

"Learn what pitch you can hit good; then wait for that pitch."

Willie Keeler

In 1958, the Red Sox featured two masters of knowing what pitch to hit. Pete Runnels (right) and Ted Williams (left) went down to the wire battling for the American League batting championship. Runnels eventually lost out, hitting .322 to Williams' .328, but he did capture two batting titles with Boston (1960 and 1962). A member of the Red Sox from 1958 to 1962, Runnels straddled the Williams and Carl Yastrzemski eras, and he is often lost to obscurity, despite compiling an impressive .320 average during his five seasons with the team.

"The Splendid Splinter"

Ted Williams demonstrating his graceful swing, May 1941

> **"Baseball gives every American boy a chance to excel, not just to be as good as someone else but to be better than someone else. This is the nature of man and the name of the game."**
>
> *Ted Williams*

Ted Williams was a hero to millions of American boys and girls who marveled at his ability to excel and be better than nearly everybody else on the baseball diamond. Widely regarded as one of the game's greatest all-time hitters, the "Splendid Splinter" was a six-time batting champ and four-time home run king who also led the league in on-base percentage a dozen times. A statue outside of Fenway Park pays homage to Williams' inspiration to a generation of young baseball fans.

"A manager who cannot get along with a .400 hitter ought to have his head examined."

Joe McCarthy, on Ted Williams

Joe McCarthy was a nine-time pennant winner as skipper of the Chicago Cubs and New York Yankees when he was hired in Boston before the 1948 season. He had managed such legends as Rogers Hornsby, Babe Ruth, Lou Gehrig, Joe DiMaggio, and others—yet, getting the chance to write into the lineup a great hitter like Ted Williams was a special treat for even an experienced manager. Although McCarthy's Sox posted 96-win seasons in 1948 and 1949, they were unable to surpass the dominating Yankees, and McCarthy was gone after a 31–28 start in 1950.

"Did they tell me how to pitch to Williams? Sure they did. It was great advice, very encouraging. They said he had no weakness, won't swing at a bad ball, has the best eyes in the business, and can kill you with one swing. He won't hit anything bad, but don't give him anything good."

Bobby Shantz, on Ted Williams

Just seeing Ted Williams in the on-deck circle was enough to make pitchers ill at ease, especially if he were protecting a narrow lead or pitching in a close the game. Williams drove in more than 1,800 runs in his career and reached base by hit or by base on balls nearly 50 percent of the time that he came to bat. From his warm-up position, Williams appears to be wielding a weapon, which a baseball bat surely was in his hands—but fortunately for Bobby Shantz and others, he was only allowed to bring one bat to the plate.

196

"The way those clubs shift against Ted Williams, I can't understand how he can be so stupid not to accept the challenge to him and hit to left field."

Ty Cobb

In July 1946, Cleveland Indians manager Lou Boudreau first employed the "Williams Shift" in an attempt to stifle Ted Williams' productivity, placing three infielders to the right of second base. Williams, a strict pull hitter, was bothered by the tactic but not, statistics show, enough to affect his hitting. Not simply stubbornness on his part, Williams' reluctance to simply push the ball to the left side of the field illustrated his basic hitting philosophy: to hit the middle of the ball as hard as he could. If he connected properly, it would, in most instances, result in a base hit without forcing him to change his swing.

"Health is a state of complete physical, mental, and social well-being, and not merely the absence of disease or infirmity."

World Health Organization, 1948

Ted Williams experienced plenty of physical and mental well-being to his Hall of Fame career, although he did struggle with injuries, particularly late in his career. After returning from the Korean War in 1953, Williams never played in more than 136 games in a season over his final seven years in the majors. In April 1959, the nurses at New England Baptist Hospital tried to help relieve his neck and shoulder pains, but the 40-year-old Williams only appeared in 103 games that season, and he posted the only sub-.300 batting average of his career.

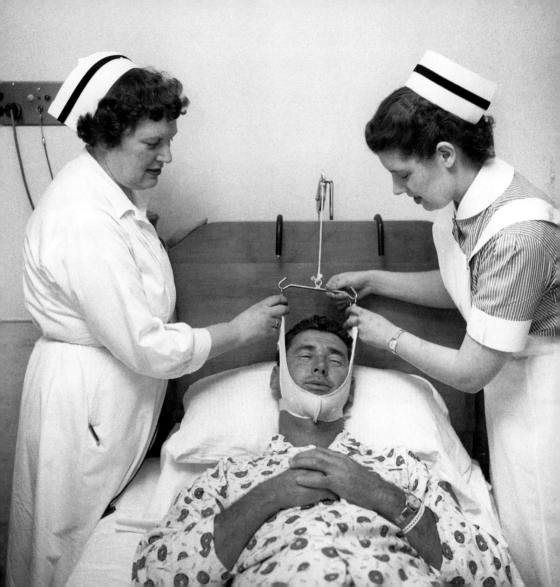

"We tell lies when we are afraid, afraid of what we don't know, afraid of what others will think, afraid of what will be found out about us. But every time we tell a lie, the thing that we fear grows stronger."

Ted Williams

On September 1, 1958, after striking out during a crucial point in a game against the Senators at Fenway Park, an enraged Ted Williams threw his bat into the stands, injuring a female spectator. Although it did not seem that Williams was a liar, he was haunted by other demons, which came bursting out at various points in his baseball career, often in explosions of anger. Maybe the fear that Williams talks of is at the heart of all lying. The suppression of that fear may give rise to all kinds of demonstrative emotions, including such tempestuous outbursts.

"Oh, I hated that Boston press. . . . I can still remember the things they wrote, and they still make me mad."

Ted Williams, in My Turn at Bat

Ted Williams hated everything about the press, including the writers and the photographers. He bemoaned how the press always claimed he wasn't a team player, that he was jealous of other players and alienated them from the reporters, and that Williams couldn't hit in the clutch. The photographers relished picturing him in various emotional states whenever possible, showing him as irascible, uncooperative, and distant. Williams was an irrepressible man and would not give the press what they wanted, but he did understand the game, both on the field and off.

"Ted was everything that was right about the game of baseball. If you really think about it, he was everything that is right about this country."

Lloyd McClendon, on Ted Williams

Not only was Ted Williams one of the best baseball players the game has ever seen, he was also a devoted patriot. He missed nearly five full seasons, in his prime, to serve his country during both World War II and the Korean War, and he never once complained about it. If you add in the numbers from those missed seasons, he might have challenged Babe Ruth's home run totals, Hank Aaron's RBI record, and almost certainly would have collected 3,000 career hits.

"They can talk about Babe Ruth and Ty Cobb and Rogers Hornsby and Lou Gehrig and Joe DiMaggio and Stan Musial and all the rest, but I'm sure not one of them could hold cards and spades to Williams in his sheer knowledge of hitting. He studied hitting the way a broker studies the stock market, and could spot at a glance mistakes that others couldn't see in a week."

Carl Yastrzemski, on Ted Williams

It must have been hard for Carl Yastrzemski to follow Ted Williams as the left fielder for the Boston Red Sox. Williams was a legend, a player everyone knew and everyone wanted to see play. Yaz was drafted by Boston in 1958 and joined the team as a 21-year-old rookie in 1961 after Williams retired. But the young Yastrzemski was able to glean some bits of wisdom from the master, who continued to work with the team as a hitting coach, as seen at spring training in 1963.

From the "Impossible Dream" to Bill "F---ing" Buckner

Carlton Fisk wills his home run into fair territory during the World Series, October 1975

"He's a dull, boring potato farmer from Long Island who just happened to be a great ballplayer. But he was the worst dresser in organized baseball."

Bill Lee, on Carl Yastrzemski

Carl Yastrzemski's off-field attire didn't interest his fans, though apparently it was a subject of ridicule for his teammates—perhaps rightly so, judging by this photo from the early 1980s. But for the Red Sox faithful, Yaz was no laughing matter, especially in 1967, when he won the American League triple crown with 44 home runs, 121 runs batted in, and a .326 batting average, and virtually carried the Sox during the stretch run. His near-perfect performance in the season's closing series against Minnesota helped the Red Sox to win both games and secure the pennant.

"All the decisive blows are struck left-handed."

Walter Benjamin

Carl Yastrzemski struck many decisive blows in his 23 seasons as a left-handed hitter for the Red Sox, and perhaps none was more significant than his three-run homer against the Minnesota Twins on September 30, 1967. The blast proved to be the game winner and brought Boston into a tie for first place with one game left to play. The Red Sox beat Minnesota again on the final day of the season to win the pennant, thanks to Yaz's four-for-four performance. In all, Yastrzemski collected seven hits and six RBI in the two-game series, helping to complete Boston's "Impossible Dream."

"The three-thousand hitting thing was the first time I let individual pressure get to me. I was uptight about it. When I saw the hit going through, I had a sigh of relief more than anything."

Carl Yastrzemski

Carl Yastrzemski admires with a sense of relief the ball he hit to right field at Fenway on September 12, 1979, to reach the 3,000-hit mark. Yaz came up to the Red Sox as a 21-year-old just after the legendary Ted Williams retired, but rather than face the pressure of trying to live up to Williamsonian expectations, he won over the fans on the merits of his own accomplishments. The 18-time all-star amassed Hall of Fame–caliber stats year after year and reached the milestone hit in his nineteenth major league season, all of which were in Boston.

"Initially, it was what you would dream about in Little League. The winning pitcher, being on the mound to win the pennant, everyone congratulating me. But a few minutes later, you realize you're not going where you want to go. I was trying to get back in the dugout. Thank God for the Boston police, they were able to control the crowd."

Jim Lonborg, on the 1967 pennant

Photographed after the final out against the Minnesota Twins on October 2, 1967, Jim Lonborg is hoisted onto his teammates' shoulders in jubilation. Lonborg got the win on the last day of the season to secure the pennant for Boston. But things quickly got a little scary on the Fenway Park field, as jubilation gave way to chaos. So goes baseball in Boston. The wild excitement continued into the World Series, where Lonborg won two postseason thrillers before losing Game Seven to the Cardinals' ace, Bob Gibson.

"The essence of romantic love is that wonderful beginning, after which sadness and impossibility may become the rule."

Anita Brookner

It was love at first sight when Tony Conigliaro burst onto the Boston baseball scene in 1964. The local kid from suburban Revere offered great baseball talent and good looks, too. As a rookie, he belted 24 home runs before a broken arm in August cut short his season. He bounced back to hit 32 homers in 1965, and the city fell in love with Conigliaro all over again. That was the wonderful beginning. In August 1967, the city experienced impossible sadness when Conigliaro was hit in the head with a fastball, after which his career gradually unraveled.

"Fear is the fundamental factor in hitting. . . . If a baseball, thrown hard, hits any part of your body, it hurts. If it hits certain vulnerable areas, like elbows, wrists, or face, it can cause broken bones and other serious injuries. . . . A thrown baseball, in short, is a missile, and an approaching missile generates a reflexive action: Get out of the way."

Leonard Koppett, in A Thinking Man's Guide to Baseball

On August 18, 1967, Tony Conigliaro was hit in the face by a pitch from Jack Hamilton of the California Angels. The ball shattered Conigliaro's jaw, forcing him to miss the rest of the season and all of the next. His eyesight was severely damaged by the blow, yet he was able to return to the lineup in 1969 and was named the American League Comeback Player of the Year. He performed even better in 1970, but the ocular problems kept mounting, and he played in only 95 more major league games. His story is one that makes all Red Sox fans wonder what might have been.

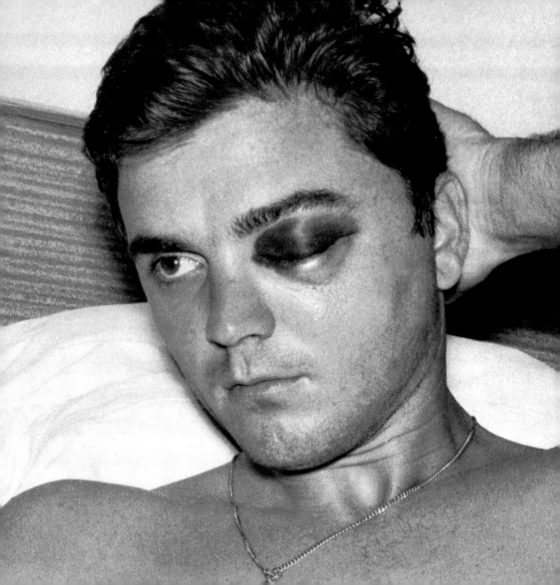

> ## "When dealing with people, remember you are not dealing with creatures of logic, but with creatures of emotion, creatures bristling with prejudice, and motivated by pride and vanity."

Dale Carnegie

Reggie Smith was a great baseball player, blessed with all the tools. Smith played more years in Boston than in any other city, and he spent his most unhappy years there, as well. Smith fell victim to the racial prejudice that was bristling in Boston at the time, and after seven good years as a Red Sox, he was ready to move on. He finished out his 17-year career with the Cardinals, Dodgers, and finally the Giants, continuing to put up all-star numbers as a dangerous switch-hitting outfielder.

> **"When you're doing it, when you're hitting home runs, you can get away with anything. But when you're not delivering, it won't work. They don't buy your act."**
>
> *Ken Harrelson*

The Red Sox organization apparently didn't buy Ken Harrelson's act during his brief stay in Boston. Although he contributed to Boston's pennant run as a late-season acquisition in 1967 and then hit 35 homers and drove in 109 runs in a full season with the club in 1968, he was traded to Cleveland just 10 games into the 1969 campaign. He had become somewhat of a hero to Boston fans, and they picketed Fenway Park to protest his unceremonious dismissal.

"I think about the cosmic snowball theory. A few million years from now the sun will burn out and lose its gravitational pull. The earth will turn into a giant snowball and be hurled through space. When that happens it won't matter if I get this guy out."

Bill Lee

Bill Lee doesn't seemed overly concerned about getting this batter out during a game against the Orioles in 1978, but he's probably not thinking about the so-called cosmic snowball theory either. Lee got a lot of guys out during his 10 seasons in Boston, and he won 17 games in three consecutive seasons (1973–1975). But more than his 94 career wins with the Red Sox, Lee is best remembered for his colorful personality and entertaining quotes.

"If the human body recognized agony and frustration, people would never run marathons, have babies, or play baseball."

Carlton Fisk

Carlton Fisk rolls on the ground after tagging out the Yankees' Thurman Munson in a home-plate collision during a 1975 game. Fisk and Munson were intense competitors and longtime foes as the top catchers in the American League while playing for the league's two fiercest teams. An 11-time all-star with Boston and later the Chicago White Sox, Fisk played more than 2,200 games behind the plate—crouching, blocking errant pitches with his body, and blockading home plate against opposing base runners—and faced plenty of both agony and frustration.

"I don't know why people like the home run so much. A home run is over as soon as it starts. . . . The triple is the most exciting play of the game. A triple is like meeting a woman who excites you, spending the evening talking and getting more excited, then taking her home. It drags on and on. You're never sure how it's going to turn out."

George Foster

Jim Rice was the rare player who could create excitement with both home runs and triples. In 1978, he belted 46 homers while thrilling the crowds with 15 three-baggers, leading the league in both categories—the last major leaguer to accomplish such a feat. It was Rice's only year atop the triples list, but he was the American League home run king three times and retired with 382 long balls, trailing only Ted Williams and Carl Yastrzemski on the all-time franchise leader board. He's sixth in Red Sox history for triples.

"I take my vote as a salute to the little guy, the one who doesn't hit 500 home runs. I was one of the guys that did all they could to win."

Joe Morgan

Jerry Remy didn't hit 500 home runs. In fact, he didn't even hit 10 home runs in 10 seasons as a major leaguer, hitting a mere two in seven years with Boston. But Remy was one of the little guys (he stood five-foot-nine, or two inches taller than Hall of Famer Joe Morgan) who did all he could to help his team. He was a good clutch hitter and bunter, and a solid fielder at the keystone position. Chronic knee problems kept Remy out of the lineup for much of his time with the Sox and ultimately shortened his career.

"Popularity is the easiest thing in the world to gain, and it is the hardest thing to hold."

Will Rogers

Big George Scott was a fan favorite at Fenway. A fun-loving, hard-hitting first baseman, Scott came up with the Red Sox in 1966 and was a starter for six seasons before being traded to Milwaukee. He returned in 1977 for two years and part of a third. Like ballplayers everywhere, when the hits were coming, Scott was popular everywhere he went, but when the production slowed down, those happy days came to an end. For the most part, he is remembered as an asset and an all-star during his time in Boston.

"Luis Tiant comes over the top, he comes sidearm, he comes three-quarters. This guy comes from everywhere but between his legs."

Curt Gowdy

The Cuban-born Luis Tiant had a unique delivery that featured all manner of gyrations and body motions, including turning his back to the batter. Every stage of his delivery was wacky; the windup, the push off, and the release point were all entertaining to the crowds who came to see him, but not much fun for the batters who had to face him. In eight seasons with the Red Sox, Tiant was a three-time 20-game winner, and he earned two victories during the 1975 World Series against Cincinnati.

"When a father gives to his son, both laugh; when a son gives to his father, both cry."

William Shakespeare

It was an emotional scene for both father and son when Luis Tiant Sr. came to Fenway Park in 1975 to throw out the ceremonial first pitch, while his son looks on. The two had not seen each other in 14 years, but the Red Sox pitcher's parents received permission from Fidel Castro to make the trip. Tiant Sr. was a star pitcher in the Cuban professional winter leagues as well as in the Negro Leagues in the United States for many years.

> **"The success of plans and the advantage to be derived from them do not at all times agree, seeing the gods claim to themselves the right to decide as to the final result."**
>
> *Marcellinus Ammianu*

Fred Lynn had an outstanding rookie year in 1975, becoming the only player ever to win the Most Valuable Player and Rookie of the Year Awards in the same season; he brought home a Gold Glove for good measure. The baseball gods were generous with the rookie Lynn, but he could never equal the performance of that inaugural season, in part because of injuries. Lynn might have felt less pressure later in his career had his rookie campaign not raised such high expectations. Early success was his curse, and his finest success was quickly behind him.

"A great catch is like watching girls go by, the last one you see is always the prettiest."

Bob Gibson

Few made prettier catches in center field than Fred Lynn in his prime. He had great instincts for covering the outfield's wide open spaces, and the jumps he could get on fly balls were startling. From 1974 to 1980 Lynn roamed the depths of Fenway's outfield, winning Gold Glove awards in 1975, 1978, 1979, and 1980. This photograph captures a marvelous full-extension, diving catch by Lynn during the 1975 World Series, showing his best on baseball's biggest stage.

"I believe in the Church of Baseball. I tried all the major religions and most of the minor ones. I've worshipped Buddha, Allah, Brahma, Vishnu, Siva, trees, mushrooms, and Isadora Duncan. I know things. For instance, there are 108 beads in a Catholic rosary and there are 108 stitches in a baseball. When I learned that, I gave Jesus a chance."

Ron Shelton, in Bull Durham

How about witchcraft? When you need some help—and the superstitious ballplayer is always in search of the extra edge—a witch might be just the thing. Here we have Bernie Carbo trying his luck with Laurie Cabot, a Salem native and practicing witch who was flown in to Cleveland on May 12, 1976, to help Carbo and the Red Sox end a 10-game losing streak. It worked. Boston defeated Cleveland 6–4 in 12 innings.

"When I was six years old."

*Wade Boggs, on when he knew he would
be a major league baseball player*

Wade Boggs must have developed his rapport with the game of baseball at a young age. He was a pure hitter from the moment he stepped into the batter's box. He hit above .300 in each of his first 10 seasons and led the American League in batting in 1983, 1985, 1986, 1987, and 1988. In addition to shooting line drives all over the yard, he drew enough walks to lead the league in on-base percentage in those same seasons, as well as 1989. Though he ended his career in other cities, Boggs will always be remembered for his hitting prowess with the Red Sox.

247

"I can't remember the last time I missed a ground ball. I'll remember that one."

Bill Buckner, on Game Six of the 1986 World Series

Few images turn a Red Sox fan's stomach more than one showing Bill Buckner in the field with a glove on his hand. It is an image seared into the minds of the Boston faithful ever since that fateful October day in 1986, when a routine ground ball off the bat of Mookie Wilson trickled through Buckner's legs and allowed the New York Mets to survive another day. Although most Red Sox fans have since forgiven Buckner (thanks in no small part to later World Series triumphs in 2004 and 2007), few will forget it.

"People always remember the last thing that happened. They don't remember the other parts of the game, that we left 14 men on base."

Bob Stanley, on Game Six of the 1986 World Series

Bill Buckner's legacy is forever tainted by his crucial blunder in the 1986 World Series, but as is often the case, others can share in the blame. Pitcher Calvin Schiraldi allowed the Mets to rally with three hits in the bottom of the tenth, and Bob Stanley (shown here after the game) let in the game-tying run from third with a wild pitch to Mookie Wilson moments before the fateful groundball to first. The Sox had plenty of chances to win Game Six, and there was still a whole other game to be played in which Buckner or any other player could have reclaimed glory for Boston.

"When I negotiated Bob Stanley's contract with the Red Sox, we had statistics demonstrating he was the third-best pitcher in the league. They had a chart showing he was the sixth-best pitcher on the Red Sox."

Bob Woolf, agent

Even though Bob Stanley was a workhorse for the Red Sox for his entire 13-year career, he did not command a very bright spotlight or the respect of the front office. What he did do is lead the major leagues in relief innings pitched in 1981, 1982, and 1983, and he still holds the franchise record for career saves. In 1978 he came out of the bullpen to post a 15–2 record and followed with 16 wins the following year. He retired in 1989 while earning just over a million dollars per year, a mere pittance by today's standards.

"Go West, young man, go West."

Horace Greeley

Bruce Hurst was one of the top southpaw pitchers in Red Sox history, along with Mel Parnell and Lefty Grove. Hurst drew a Red Sox salary for his first nine seasons in the majors, and he won at least 11 games every year from 1983 through 1988. He timed his best season well, winning 18 games in the final year under contract just before becoming a free agent after the 1988 season. Though at age 30 no longer a young man, Hurst chose to go west to San Diego, even though the Red Sox offered him more money.

> ## "I'm cocky, I guess. . . . Baseball got in me when I was little. It runs in my family, and it rubbed off on me. It's a disease. I'm never gonna get discouraged. Puzzled sometimes, but never down. Never."
>
> *Dennis "Oil Can" Boyd*

Oil Can Boyd may have been a little discouraged after getting tagged for six runs in seven innings during Game Three of the 1986 World Series against the Mets. The lanky righty had posted a career-high 16 wins during the regular season and earned a key victory in the League Championship Series, but after 1986, Boyd's stats tumbled and his fastball slowed. He remained in the big leagues through 1991, finishing his career with Montreal and Texas.

"I am intense, no question about it. Every time I toe the rubber, it's no different for me than it was in the World Series. That might be somebody's only chance to see me pitch. They might have driven four hours to get there. I'm going to be out there if I can help it."

Roger Clemens

No one has questioned Roger Clemens' intensity. On the mound, Clemens could lock himself into a kind of tunnel vision, blocking out extraneous sensory information, or so it appeared. Whether he was truly concerned about that faithful fan or not, he had the ability to convert his single-minded purpose into a winning strategy. He was intense when he trained, he was intense when he studied hitters, and he was intense whenever he took the mound.

"I wish (Hank Aaron) were still playing. I'd probably crack his head open to show him how valuable I was."

Roger Clemens

Roger Clemens didn't take too kindly to Hank Aaron's comment that pitchers should not be allowed to win the Most Valuable Player Award because they don't play every day. Although Clemens' response betrays both a lack of decorum and a sense of perspective, when channeled to the playing field, his passion resulted in success. In 1986, he recorded league-high marks of 24 wins and a 2.48 while helping to lead the Red Sox to a pennant, earning him not only the Cy Young Award but also American League Most Valuable Player honors.

> ## "I read where Roger Clemens said (making the Hall of Fame) was a goal of his. To me, that's like planning for the ninth inning when you're in the first."

Jim Palmer, after being elected to the Hall of Fame in 1990

Roger Clemens never lacked confidence. When he was just 21 and new to the big leagues, he loved to win and worked fiendishly at it, and the fans loved him for it. But after a 24-year career, Clemens' entry into the Hall of Fame depends less on his statistics, his awards, or his World Series rings, and more on how his legacy is perceived by the sportswriters and people like Jim Palmer. Clemens seems to be getting along well with Hall of Famer Tom Seaver after receiving his second Cy Young Award, in 1988.

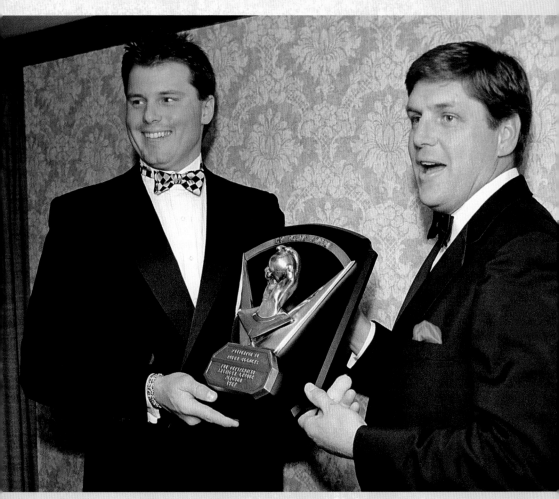

> "It's been said before, but it's true: For Red Sox fans, watching Roger Clemens thrive as a Yankee is the equivalent of watching your ex-wife marry your sworn mortal enemy—then live happily ever after."

Sportswriter Sean McAdam

Red Sox fans believed they owned Roger Clemens. After all, he came up in Boston, became a star in Boston, gained national attention in Boston, and was the number one pitcher in the rotation there for 13 seasons. With this sense of Clemens as New England property, what could have been crueler than his signing a contract with the despised New York Yankees? What was worse was that he pitched so well in the Big Apple, winning awards, setting records, and earning a World Series ring in pinstripes.

> # "Who can guess how much industry and providence and affection we have caught from the pantomime of brutes?"

Ralph Waldo Emerson

The powerful Mo Vaughn was no brute, but he gained much affection during his seven and a half seasons with the Red Sox. He hit home runs at a rate of once every 16.6 at bats; only David Ortiz, Manny Ramirez, Jimmie Foxx, and Ted Williams hit long balls at a more proficient rate for Boston. Vaughn won the American League Most Valuable Player Award in 1995 with 39 homers, 126 RBI, and a .300 average. He improved in nearly every offensive category in 1996, batting .326 while posting career highs of 44 home runs, 143 RBI, 118 runs, 207 hits, and 95 walks.

"If you have a success, you have it for the wrong reasons. If you become popular, it is always because of the worst aspects of your work."

Ernest Hemingway

Nomar Garciaparra was very popular during his eight years in Boston, and it was always for the right reasons—his clutch hitting, his slick fielding, and his all-around good nature. Other than the injury-shortened 2001 season, Garciaparra batted over .300 every year he played in Boston, and he won American League batting crowns in 1999 and 2000. Unfortunately, "No-mah" didn't get to partake in the team's success, as he was shipped to the Cubs in a deadline-day trade in July 2004.

"In retrospect, you are always looking back."

Jimy Williams

Red Sox fans look back on manager Jimy Williams as the man who *almost* got them there. In 1998, Williams guided the Sox to 92 wins and a second-place finish. A year later, the team posted another second-place result, and in 2000, Williams' Sox finished at 85–77, good enough once again for second place. He was fired in mid-August of 2001, with the Sox sitting (where else?) in second place with a 65–53 record. All in all, his lifetime record with Boston was 414–352, a very respectable .540 winning percentage—but he could never take them to the promised land.

The Return of the Boston Dynasty

Champions!! The 2007 Boston Red Sox

"Pressure is a word that is misused in our vocabulary. When you start thinking of pressure, it's because you've started to think of failure."

Tommy Lasorda

The Red Sox players were surely feeling the pressure after losing the first three games of the 2004 American League Championship Series to the New York Yankees—but failure was the furthest thing from their minds. After a 19–8 trouncing in Game Three at home, the Sox bounced back to win a 12-inning thriller the next night. It took 14 innings to eke out a victory in Game Five, and then the Red Sox went on to defy the odds by winning Games Six and Seven at Yankee Stadium. The pressure-free Sox went on to sweep St. Louis in the World Series.

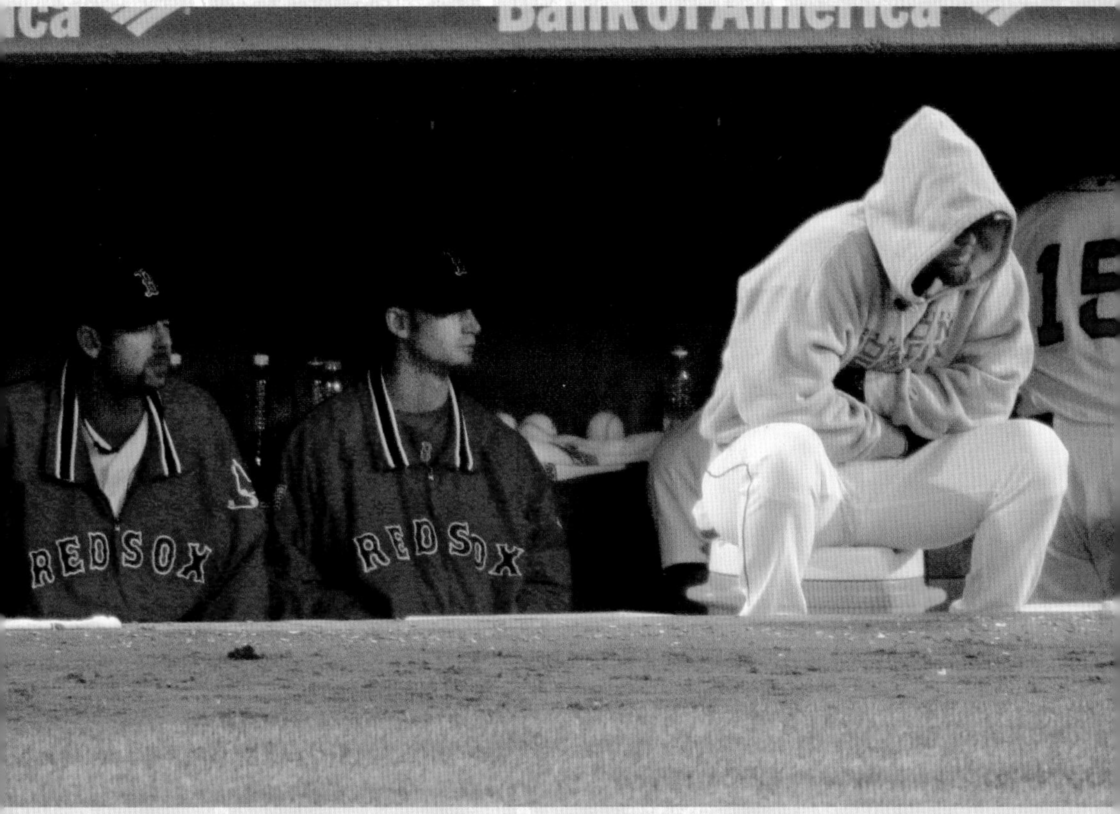
REDSOX
REDSOX
15

> **"Catching is much like managing. Managers don't really win games, but they can lose plenty of them. The same with catching. If you're doing a quality job, you should be almost anonymous."**
>
> *Bob Boone*

Unlike catchers, though, managers usually don't have to worry about being run over by players charging full speed from third base toward home. In addition to his toughness blocking the plate, Jason Varitek has been efficient and reliable behind the plate for more than a decade, calling games, handling the Red Sox pitching staff, and helping the team win plenty of games. As the team captain, Varitek leads by example, even if his relative anonymity keeps him out of the headlines and in the shadows of some of his flashier teammates.

"I just try to do what I have to do and let the people out there do what they have to do, which is have fun, scream, yell, and jump around. I try to do what I have to do, which is play baseball, and I can only play in that piece of area there, so that's what I try to do."

Pedro Martinez

Pedro Martinez is a loveable guy, and Red Sox fans loved him—as long as he was healthy and winning games for Boston. A colorful character with a fastball that pops, Martinez brings fans to the ballpark wherever he pitches. And just like the crowds in Los Angeles and Montreal before them, the Fenway Park fans welcomed him with great enthusiasm and hope. There is no doubt that Pedro notices the jumping, screaming, and yelling and uses it to fuel his intensity. He plays on his little piece of area and entertains an entire stadium.

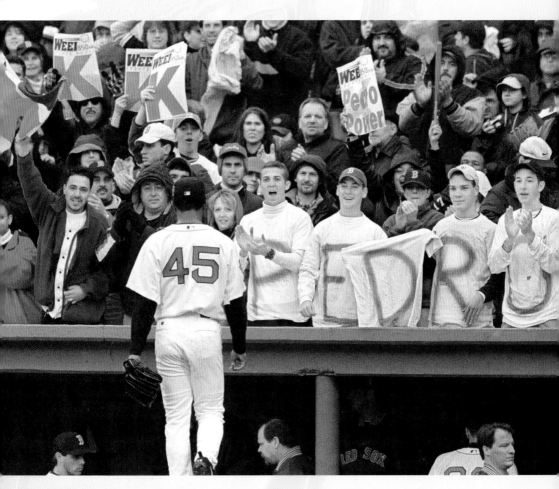

> "I felt the power in my fastball. . . . That's probably why I left so many fastballs up. I was a little more erratic. I just couldn't get the ball over."

Pedro Martinez

When Pedro's fastball is on and he is hitting his spots, he is unhittable. He has a flex in his arm that gives the appearance of a slingshot when he releases the ball, which only makes it harder to connect with his 90-plus-mph heater. Martinez's greatest difficulty during his time in Boston came from brief episodes of wildness, which usually occurred in the middle innings of ball games. He sometimes couldn't locate his fastball, and the batters' ability to take advantage often made the difference between winning and losing.

"If a no-hitter comes, I'll take it. I don't go out there expecting no-hitters, but I was lucky enough to be flirting with a no-hitter today. I'm just proud I was able to come here and show the fans what I didn't have enough time to show them before."

Pedro Martinez, in 2004

Pedro Martinez showed fans plenty during his seven seasons in Boston, although pitching a no-hitter was one of the few achievements he didn't meet. A five-time all-star and two-time Cy Young Award winner with the Red Sox, Martinez led the American League in ERA four times and in strikeouts three times between 1998 and 2004. His combined 41–10 record, 1.90 ERA, and 597 strikeouts over 1999 and 2000 is one of the best back-to-back seasons any pitcher has put forth in the modern era.

"We've seen it so often. The whole inning we're sitting there thinking, 'Let's just get David to the plate.' He just has the ability to take such good swings in those situations. He doesn't do anything different. I think he's smart enough to know the pressure is on the other team, even though we're down."

Manager Terry Francona, on David Ortiz

When you look at David "Big Papi" Ortiz swinging, you realize not only what a large plate area his bat can cover, but also what a tremendous amount of torque his long swing can generate. He loves to come to bat in pressure-packed situations, displaying the confidence of a slugger. With his long reach and experience in tight-game situations, quite a few pitchers leave the mound disappointed.

"Obviously . . . he's a freak. He's like a superhero. He's like that in real life, too, and I think that's why everything about him is so endearing, because he is a genuine person and people here love him, and there's a reason why."

Josh Beckett, on David Ortiz

David Ortiz got freaky in the Red Sox clubhouse after the team clinched a playoff spot in September 2008. Ortiz's combination of athletic giant and gentle, personable man endears him to both the press and the public, and his monstrous accomplishments at the plate have caught the attention of the nation. He led the league in RBI in 2005 and 2006, and his 54 homers in 2006 rank as the highest single-season total in Red Sox history.

287

"After I got to Boston and started playing for the Red Sox, I would walk around the clubhouse and talk to guys, and I starting calling them *papi*. . . . In the Dominican Republic, we use the word all the time, like Americans would use "buddy" or "pal," but it's more like "daddy" or "pops." . . . And it wasn't too long before the name somehow belonged to me."

David Ortiz

David Ortiz is really big, and he's really nice, and fans young and old love him. He's their baseball father, the man who helps the family stick together. He has earned the respect of baseball writers as well, who have selected him as one of the American League's five most valuable players in each of his first five seasons in Boston, although "Big Papi" has yet to bring home an MVP trophy.

"You might well be looking at a guy who will surpass 600 home runs, 2,000 RBI, and a .300 batting average by the time he retires. But let's not wait to celebrate the greatness in our midst. Even today, Ramirez can make a case to be among the five greatest right-handed hitters of all time."

Tom Verducci, on Manny Ramirez

Manny Ramirez is a pure hitter. He's also different, creative, and eccentric—and perhaps some other less flattering adjectives, in the eyes of opposing players and fans. But if you look beyond his antics, it is hard to deny that he is one of the game's great hitters. In his seven full seasons in Boston (2001–2007), he was selected to the all-star team seven times and earned six Silver Slugger Awards. He ranks in the top-ten among all active players in batting average, home runs, RBI, runs scored, slugging percentage, on-base percentage, and walks.

"If there's anyone who should be careful not to invite dumb blond jokes, it's Manny Ramirez. But that's what he's done with a combination of his tinted locks, sluggish bat, shaky glove, and curious case of sore calves. It is possible that Ramirez strained his calves while lifting weights, as he says. . . . But Manny being Manny, there could be any number of explanations, short of him moonlighting with the Rockettes. Not his kind of music."

Bud Shaw, Cleveland Plain Dealer

The origins of "Manny being Manny" trace back to Cleveland, where Manny Ramirez got his start in the major leagues, and his wacky view of the world and of the game he plays so well has since become part of the national baseball consciousness. His unexplained disappearances, his outbursts on and off the field, his unorthodox play in the outfield, and his non-conformist appearance all are part of his story. Although his relationship with the Red Sox came to a rocky end in 2008, Ramirez was an integral part of the team's success for many years.

293

"I don't believe in accidents. There are only encounters in history. There are no accidents."

Pablo Picasso

When outfielder Johnny Damon collided with infielder Damien Jackson during Game Five of the 2003 American League Division Series against Oakland, it was more than just an encounter. They both ended up prone on the grass, and Damon had to be taken off the field in an ambulance. He suffered a concussion, but the Sox went on to win the clinching game, and Damon was back in the lineup for the start of the League Championship Series against New York.

> # "I've always believed that it's important to show a new look periodically. Predictability can lead to failure."

T. Boone Pickens

Johnny Damon sported a new, hairy look in 2004, earning him the nickname "Caveman." He was also a key component of the self-described "Idiots" that came back in dramatic fashion to beat the Yankees in the League Championship Series before going on to win the first World Series for the Red Sox since 1918. Here he poses in May 2004, right before having his beard shaved for a charity event in Boston.

"Each player must accept the cards life deals him or her; but once they are in hand, he or she alone must decide how to play the cards in order to win the game."

Voltaire

While each of these Red Sox had to decide how to play his own cards during a clubhouse game of cribbage prior to an interleague contest at San Francisco in June 2004, they didn't have to do it alone on the playing field. The team went on to win 98 games during the regular season and went 11–3 in the postseason to win the championship.

"It's time for me to cowboy up."

Kevin Millar

It's October 24, 2004, and Kevin Millar has cowboyed up. He just scored a key run against the St. Louis Cardinals in Game Two of the World Series, and he is being mobbed by his exuberant teammates—Millar's face can be seen amidst the sea of red jackets. Millar's catch phrase became a catalyst for the Sox's stretch drive and the battle cry for the series. Millar spent only three seasons in Boston, playing mostly first base and outfield, but his impact on the 2004 championship squad resonated throughout New England.

"The will is a beast of burden. If God mounts it, it wishes and goes as God wills; if Satan mounts it, it wishes and goes as Satan wills; nor can it choose its rider. . . . The riders contend for its possession."

Martin Luther

Curt Schilling was a beast of burden for the Red Sox and every other team he pitched for during his long career. He was also a willful pitcher, winning important games through determination and grit. He led the Red Sox with 21 wins in 2004 and, shortly after undergoing ankle surgery, pitched Boston to victory in Game Six of that year's League Championship Series against the Yankees—resulting in Schilling's now-legendary bloody sock. The will didn't choose to ride Schilling, but the pitcher surely possessed it.

> ## "When you're out there in the big league pressure cooker, a pitcher's attitude—his utter confidence that he has an advantage of will and luck and guts over the hitter—is almost as important as his stuff."
>
> *Bill Veeck*

Few pitchers in recent years have demonstrated the combination of confidence, will, and guts in the postseason pressure cooker more than Josh Beckett. After helping the Florida Marlins win a title in 2003, Beckett came to Boston in 2006 and proved instrumental in the run for the championship in 2007. He pitched a complete-game shutout against the Angels in the League Division Series, earned two victories against Cleveland in the League Championship Series, and showed his stuff with a Game One win in the World Series (shown here).

"There are two theories on hitting the knuckleball. Unfortunately, neither of them work."

Charlie Lau

Hitters have been trying to develop a theory on how to hit Tim Wakefield's knuckleballs for more than a decade. Throwing the knuckleball takes a soft touch combined with rapid arm movement, perfect timing, and an understanding of the structure of the ball. Not many pitchers can throw this pitch effectively, but Wakefield has become a master. Since 1995, hitters who come to town for a four-game series against the Red Sox have to contend with the unpredictable knuckleball after three days of rockets from Boston's other hurlers.

"The best way to catch a knuckleball is to wait until the ball stops rolling and then pick it up."

Bob Uecker

Bob Uecker never caught Tim Wakefield, but the former big league backstop understands the challenges of receiving the knuckler. Doug Mirabelli, shown here chatting with Wakefield during a game in 2006, was Wakefield's designated catcher for most of the knuckleballer's time in Boston. Like most knuckleball catchers, Mirabelli donned a special oversized mitt for the task of reining in the unpredictable flutterball. Well over 80 percent of Wakefield's pitches are knucklers, and because it is easy on the arm, Wakefield should have a spot on a major league roster for years to come.

"It was like boxing with your hands tied behind your back. You look like you're trying to catch a butterfly with a waffle iron."

Josh Bard, on Tim Wakefield's knuckleball

Josh Bard was acquired by Boston prior to the 2006 season to serve as a backup catcher. Within the first month of the season, Bard had four passed balls in one game and ten passed balls in four games while catching Tim Wakefield. On May 1, 2006, Bard was sent packing to San Diego in exchange for Doug Mirabelli, who had been Wakefield's catcher for years before being traded to San Diego the previous December. Mirabelli remained with Boston through the 2007 season, when Kevin Cash took over the task of attempting to catch Wakefield's butterfly.

> **"Sure I am this day we are masters of our fate, that the task which has been set before us is not above our strength; that its pangs and toils are not beyond our endurance. As long as we have faith in our own cause and an unconquerable will to win, victory will not be denied us."**
>
> *Winston Churchill*

Although his numbers are not as gaudy as some of his teammates', Mike Lowell is a master of his fate. The quiet veteran understands the task at hand and exhibits a will to win, a will that helped the Florida Marlins win the World Series in 2003 and the Red Sox do it in 2007. In 2007, he batted .400 and drove in four runs in the four-game sweep of the Colorado Rockies, earning him the World Series Most Valuable Player Award. Here he slides home with a run in the clinching fourth game.

"If you're not a good hitter, you're not going to walk. I mean, you'll find most of the guys that have the most walks are pretty good hitters. Otherwise, the pitchers would throw it right down the middle every time."

Kevin Youkilis

Kevin Youkilis—Boston's intense first baseman—worked harder as a student of hitting than most people give him credit for. Smart and selective at the plate, he earned 91 bases on balls in his first full major league season in 2006 and posted a .390 on-base percentage in 2007 and 2008. In this photo, he gets a pitch right down the middle during the 2008 League Championship Series and drives it into the seats for a home run. Youkilis' energy and gung-ho attitude quickly made him a fan favorite in Boston.

"If I had to name the number one asset you could have for any sport, I'd say speed. In baseball, all a guy with speed has to do is make contact."

Ron Fairly

Over the years, speedsters have been a rarity in Boston. With a few exceptions—such as Tommy Harper in the early 1970s and Johnny Damon in the early 2000s—Red Sox lineups have been built on power and hitting since the end of the dead-ball era. Jacoby Ellsbury is bucking that trend. In his first full season, in 2008, Ellsbury became only the third Red Sox player to steal 50 bases in a season (the others are Harper and Tris Speaker). The young outfielder also used his speed to get on base and track down fly balls in the field.

"Baseball's future? Bigger and bigger, better, and better! No question about it, it's the greatest game there is!"

Ted Williams

Bigger truly is better when it comes in a package like Jonathan Papelbon. Out of Pawtucket came the bullpen savior for the Red Sox, and Boston rode him all the way to victory in the 2007 World Series. At 6-foot-4 and 230 pounds, Papelbon uses his size to overpower hitters in the late innings of ball games. Though Ted Williams likely was not predicting the increasing size of major league closers, he was right on target about baseball being the greatest game there is.

> **"If this humor be the safety of our race, then it is due largely to the infusion into the American people of the Irish brain."**
>
> *William Howard Taft*

Ever since he first arrived in Boston in 2005, Jonathan Papelbon exhibited an appreciation for humor and for Boston's Irish influences. His Riverdance-like celebratory jigs, his victory cigars, and his leprechaun face all quickly endeared him to the Red Sox faithful—especially when it came in the wake of the pennant victory in 2007. A ham to say the least, the flame-throwing relief pitcher was not shy about showing off his dance moves in front of the cameras and the crowds.

"Look in the mirror, and don't be tempted to equate transient domination with either intrinsic superiority or prospects for extended survival."

Stephen Jay Gould

Jason Varitek, reflected in a mirror during spring training in 2007, knew there was nothing intrinsic about the Red Sox's success. Beginning in the late 1990s, the Boston Red Sox were about as dominant as any other baseball team. With six postseason berths between 1998 and 2008, the Red Sox were the first franchise to earn two championships in the new century when they won the 2004 and 2007 World Series. But with decades of frustration behind them, few Boston players or fans were tempted to equate victory with intrinsic superiority.

> **"These are days when no one should rely unduly on his competence. Strength lies in improvisation."**
>
> *Walter Benjamin*

First baseman Kevin Youkilis and second baseman Dustin Pedroia appear to be improvising in their attempt to snare a foul pop-up during the 2007 American League Championship Series in Cleveland, but competency is what got them there. These two infielders were vital pieces on the World Series champions that won 96 games during the regular season and posted the second-highest team fielding percentage in the league. The Red Sox also produced the third-most runs on offense, and the Boston pitching staff posted the AL's lowest ERA.

Skippers and the Men in Blue

Manager Terry Francona airs his grievance with umpire Greg Gibson, April 2005

> "Learn the fundamentals. Study and work at the game as if it were a science. Keep in top physical condition. Make yourself as effective as possible. Get the desire to win. Keeping in the best physical condition and having an intense spirit to succeed is the combination for winning games."

Ty Cobb

Manager Terry Francona (background, far left) tries to instill the fundamentals in his players during spring training at Fort Myers, Florida, in February 2007. A desire to win, an intense spirit to succeed, and good physical conditioning combined to help the Red Sox win the World Series that season. It is a formula that has worked well for Francona's clubs since he took the managerial job in 2004.

"When you're finished changing, you're finished."

Benjamin Franklin

Joe Cronin sits alone in the Boston dugout during spring training circa 1936, perhaps contemplating what changes lay ahead. After seven years with the Washington Senators—including the last two as both shortstop and manager—he changed directions in 1935 to assume the dual role with Boston. After the Sox landed in third place in 1947, one year removed from a pennant, Cronin was finished as a big league manager. But more changes lay ahead, as he spent 11 seasons as the team's general manager before taking a turn as president of the American League from 1959 to 1973.

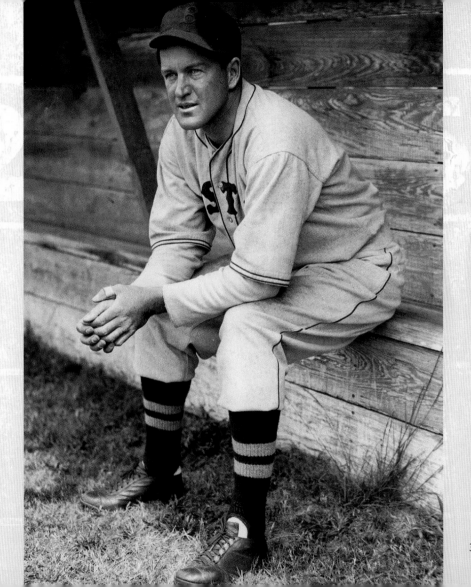

331

"Managing a ball club is the most vulnerable job in the world. From the moment you take the job you're vulnerable. If you don't win, you're going to be fired. If you do win, you've only put off the day you're going to be fired."

Leo Durocher, in Nice Guys Finish Last

Grady Little, seen here surrounded by media during the 2003 League Championship Series, wasn't able to put off the day he was fired much longer. His decision to leave Pedro Martinez on the mound into the eighth inning of Game Seven against the Yankees proved disastrous, as the Red Sox blew a 4–0 lead before ultimately losing in 11 innings. Little won 93 and 95 games in 2002 and 2003, respectively, finishing second to New York both times—but they would be his only two seasons as the Boston skipper.

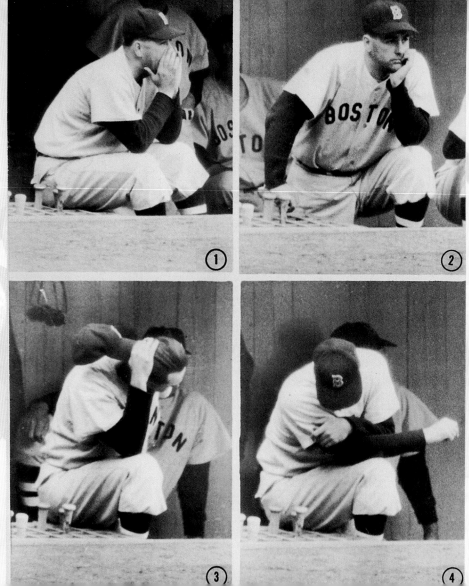

"All managers are losers. They are the most expendable pieces of furniture on the face of the earth."

Ted Williams

Lou Boudreau led Cleveland to its last World Series victory in 1948, but after coming over to Boston in 1952, Boudreau quickly proved expendable. After three seasons finishing no closer than 16 games out of first place (and 42 games out in 1954), Boudreau was fired. During his tenure, however, he was denied the team's greatest star, as Ted Williams spent much of the time in military service or injured. In this photo, Boudreau watches in agony as the New York Yankees score 11 runs in one inning during a game in May 1952. The Red Sox lost 18–3.

"Most managers are lifetime .220 hitters. For years, pitchers have been getting these managers out 75 percent of the time, and that's why they don't like us."

Bill Lee

Manager Don Zimmer never did particularly like Bill Lee, his eccentric pitcher. Zimmer was called "Old Buffalo Head" by disgruntled players, who saw him as rigid and short-sighted in how he handled the team personnel. With Zimmer as skipper from 1976 to 1980, the Red Sox won more than 90 games three times but never reached higher than second place in the standings. Some argued that, with the talent it had, Boston could have finished in first place *without* a manager. For the record, Zimmer was a lifetime .235 hitter during his 12-year playing career.

"I hope he doesn't yell at me like I used to yell at my managers."

Bob Stanley, on coaching his son's little league team

Bill Lee used to yell at his managers, too, especially when that manager was Don Zimmer. Zim was at the helm for one of the biggest collapses in baseball history, when the Red Sox squandered a huge midseason advantage over the Yankees in 1978. In the heat of the pennant race that September, Zimmer refused to pitch Lee, who was known as the staff Yankee killer, in a crucial four-game series against New York. Instead, Zim went with rookie Bobby Sprowl, who was knocked out of the box in four innings, and Boston's swoon continued.

"If trying to treat the players as human beings is spoiling them, then I spoil them. But I was brought up to treat a human being as a human being until he proves unworthy of himself."

Tom Yawkey

Red Sox owner Tom Yawkey was not only fair with his players, but in an era of owner tightwads, he paid them well. Yawkey was born into money and used part of the proceeds from his business empire to purchase the Red Sox for $1.5 million in 1933. He reconstructed Fenway Park with another $1.5 million and launched a new era in Boston baseball. The long-suffering fans appreciated his dedication to bringing a winner to Boston, and all were rewarded with a pennant in 1946. Here the owner talks with his manager, Joe Cronin, and Detroit Tigers manager Mickey Cochrane at spring training in 1936.

"The job of arguing with the umpire belongs to the manager, because it won't hurt the team if he gets thrown out of the game."

Earl Weaver, Hall of Fame manager

Jimy Williams lets his displeasure be known after getting ejected for arguing with the umpire during Game Four of the American League Championship Series against the Yankees in 1999. The Red Sox were losing 9–2 at that point, so the manager's ejection couldn't hurt the team any more than they had already hurt themselves. Williams had a frustrating turn as Boston's manager from 1997 to 2001, earning four straight second-place finishes and posting a 5–9 record in the postseason.

> **"Despite all the nasty things I have said about umpires, I think they're 100 percent honest, but I can't for the life of me figure out how they arrive at some of their decisions."**
>
> *Jimmy Dykes, Athletics manager*

Joe Cronin would certainly agree with Jimmy Dykes, at least the part about not understanding umpires. Cronin looks genuinely angry about a decision that has just been made. His fists are clenched, his jaw is set, and his voice surely is seething with disdain and unpleasantness. But, this is the manager's job: to clench fists, set his jaw, and seethe when the time is right and game events demand it. Cronin was not known for his temper, but years of frustration certainly gave him ample opportunity to develop it.

> ## "Many fans look upon an umpire as a necessary evil to the luxury of baseball, like the odor that follows an automobile."

Christy Mathewson

Not only do fans often take Christy Mathewson's view of an umpire, but managers, coaches, and players do, too. Here we have a full-scale fight with the umpiring crew during a July 1948 game at Briggs Stadium in Detroit. Hot under the collar are Boston manager Joe McCarthy (left) with fists clenched, Bobby Doerr (center) looking left at the gesticulating umpire, Johnny Pesky (to Doerr's right), and Dom DiMaggio (facing right). Chances are good the Sox did not win this argument, but McCarthy at least was able to have his say.

"Good leaders are like baseball umpires; they go practically unnoticed when doing their jobs right."

Byrd Baggett

Doug Griffin, Red Sox second baseman back in 1972, has just been tagged out at the plate and is sitting on his butt in a cloud of dust with Yankee catcher Thurman Munson on top of him. He's looking up at umpire Larry Barnett, who is making his presence known with a wildly animated call. Griffin had worked hard to get around the bases in an attempt to score a run, and the umpire is practically rubbing his bad fortune right in his face. Even Munson seems to be a little taken aback by Barnett's theatrics.

The Green Cathedrals

Glorious Fenway Park at night

"You should enter a ballpark the way you enter a church."

Bill Lee

Fans have been making the pilgrimage to Fenway Park for nearly a century, and seeing the park for the first time can be like a religious experience. Fenway is a destination for fans from all over the country who want to experience the unique qualities of this classic ballpark for themselves. The quirky park is like no other ballpark in the nation, and many idols of the baseball realm have graced its lush green fields.

Boston's Huntington Avenue Grounds, shown here in 1903 action, was built in 1901 to house the city's new baseball club. There were no domes to worry about, and the only visual effect at this stadium was the movement of the players. The grandstands and bleachers could accommodate between 11,000 and 12,000 fans, and despite Tom Boswell's assertion that smaller is better than bigger, the popularity of the team necessitated the move to the bigger and more modern Fenway Park in 1912.

"Several rules of stadium building should
be carved on every owner's forehead. Old, if properly
refurbished, is always better than new. Smaller is better
than bigger. Open is better than closed. Near beats far.
Silent visual effects are better than loud ones. Eye
pollution hurts attendance. Inside should look as good
as outside. Domed stadiums are criminal."

Tom Boswell, in How Life Imitates the World Series

"Out with the old, in with the new."

Anonymous

After 11 seasons at Huntington Avenue Grounds, the Red Sox moved out of the old and into the new in April 1912, beginning a glorious era at Fenway Park. The brand-new ballpark offered considerable luxuries compared to its predecessor, and it could accommodate many more fans. Built of brick, steel, and concrete, it was a sturdy structure that blended effectively into its Boston neighborhood. Still standing more than nine decades later, Fenway has been kept fresh through various renovations, but it remains the classic American ballpark well into the twenty-first century.

"It is important to realize that determinism does not imply events occur in spite of our actions. Some events occur because we determine them. Determinism must not be confused with the doctrine of fatalism, which asserts that future events are entirely beyond our control."

Paul Davies

The coziness of Fenway Park is evident when viewed from above, and even more so from inside the enclosure. The very nature of the Red Sox home, nestled into its tight urban surroundings, often determined the team's fate, whether the result of Boston lineups built solely around exploiting the field's dimensions or of an opponent's ability to take advantage of those same traits. The events determined by the Green Monster looming in left field were not always in the Red Sox's control, but they did foster a sense of fatalism in the Red Sox Nation.

"At the crack of the bat, you'd turn and run up it. Then you had to pick up the ball and decide whether to jump, go right or left, or rush down again. It took plenty of practice. They made a mountain goat out of me."

Duffy Lewis, on "Duffy's Cliff" at Fenway Park

Left fielder Duffy Lewis, one-third of Boston's "Million Dollar Outfield," was referring to the sloped outfield at Fenway Park, where he played from the year the park opened in 1912 until he was traded to the Yankees in 1918. The slope, which is apparent at the base of the wall in this photo from 1918, provided many adventures for visiting outfielders. Lewis became such a master at negotiating the slope's challenges that it was named in his honor as "Duffy's Cliff." The slope was removed during a subsequent ballpark renovation.

"Nothing is irreparable in politics."

Jean Anouilh

After Fenway Park was ravaged by fire in January 1934, the repairs began almost immediately, thanks to the quick action of politicians and unions. Although the inferno, which started mysteriously beneath the outfield bleachers, destroyed a large section of the structure, contractors worked fast to ensure that the park would be ready by opening day, a mere four months away. By April 17, the refurbished ballpark was open for business, with concrete bleachers replacing the old, flammable wooden bleachers and a new, more durable sheet-metal wall in left field—which would later be painted green.

> **"The ballpark is the star. . . . A crazy-quilt violation of city planning principles, an irregular pile of architecture, a menace to marketing consultants, Fenway Park works. It works as a symbol of New England's pride, as a repository of evergreen hopes, as a tabernacle of lost innocence. It works as a place to watch baseball."**

Martin F. Nolan

Boston fans love Fenway Park, quirks and all, and they have loved it through thick and thin. Obstructed views, long lines at the rest rooms and concessions stands, and the difficulty of securing a ticket to get into the 39,000-seat facility might discourage some fans from even attempting to see a game in person. But not Red Sox fans, who come from throughout New England to cheer on their team with pride and purpose inside this irregular pile of architecture.

"**Fenway is special precisely because it has what modern stadiums lack: seats that, while often cramped, offer the best views in baseball; and the sense that, if you squint, that could be Smoky Joe Wood pitching to Ty Cobb out there instead of Jeff Fassero and Bobby Higginson.**"

Neil deMause, sportsjones.com

The intimacy and age of Fenway Park, while denying the team some of the revenue-generating benefits of lavish suites and high-end dining, are what makes it special for millions of baseball fans season after season. The ballpark's continuity through the ages evokes the tradition and pastoral quality of the game of baseball.

> **"There are reasons why you sometimes think a player will perform better for you than for the club he's with. Usually it has to do with the architecture of your park."**
>
> *Bill Veeck, in* Veeck as in Wreck

Many Red Sox managers over the decades have surely fantasized about building a team of right-handed hitters who would bang the ball off the left wall, hitting double after single after double. The Green Monster has long been a focal point of Fenway Park, but ironically, many of Boston's greatest hitters—Williams, Yaz, Boggs, Ortiz, to name a few—hit from the left side of the plate. Among the notable exceptions was Jim Rice, who drove balls into and over the Green Monster for 16 seasons. Here the Kansas City Royals deploy a shift on the pull-hitting Rice, with three outfielders stationed in front of the Green Monster.

> **"There's nothing in the world like the fatalism of the Red Sox fans, which has been bred into them for generations by that little green ballpark, and *the wall*, and by a team that keeps trying to win by hitting everything out of sight and just out-bombarding everyone else in the league. All this makes Boston fans a little crazy, and I'm sorry for them."**

Bill Lee, in Late Innings *by Roger Angell*

Boston fans could get a new perspective on the little green ballpark beginning in 2003, when a new seating section was installed atop *the wall* in left field. The Red Sox faithful did get even crazier in 2004—but don't feel sorry for them, as the team's long-awaited championship that season turned the fatalism of the fans around for good.

"Do they leave it there during the game?"

Bill Lee, on Fenway's Green Monster

As tempting a target as the Green Monster is for right-handed batters, it is equally ominous—perhaps more so—for left-handed pitchers standing on the mound at Fenway. To newcomers, the giant green surface almost looks like a temporary structure left over from an incomplete construction job. But the Red Sox have left "it" there in left field for decades. After the 1934 fire, the original 37-foot-tall wooden wall was replaced by a metal version, which was plastered with advertisements before receiving a green paint job in 1947.

"We love Fenway Park because we love antiques, be they rocking chairs or ballparks. But we love it even more because the eccentricities of the place mirror our own. It is, like us, difficult and cranky. . . . Players come and go, but Fenway Park may become an American Pyramid."

Clark Booth, Boston Red Sox sportscaster

Not only is Fenway loved for its antiquity and its quirkiness, but also for the ghosts it contains. The ectoplasm of countless baseball stars and journeymen lives there, and the memories of intense competitions past underlie all the ball games that are played there today, as if one game is built on another, with even the roots of the grass holding knowledge about the national pastime.

From Royal Rooters to the Red Sox Nation

Souvenir program for Cy Young tribute at Huntington Avenue Grounds, August 1908

ALL UP FOR "CY"
BOSTON AMERICAN
LEAGUE GROUNDS
AUG, 13, 1908

> **"The Red Sox are a religion. Every year we re-enact the agony and the temptation in the garden. Baseball child's play? Hell, up here in Boston it's a passion play."**
>
> *George V. Higgins*

Jim Pagliaroni was in his only first full season with the Red Sox in 1961 when he got a firsthand look at the religious nature of the franchise and its fans. Here "Pag" poses with two Franciscan sisters who were among hundreds of Roman Catholic nuns attending a game at Fenway Park as guests of Cardinal Cushing—but even fans less devoted to the church are deeply devoted to their Sox. George Higgins was a Texas native whose son, Pinky Higgins, spent two and a half seasons with the Red Sox, which was plenty of time to experience the agony and the temptation of the Red Sox.

> "A large part of the hold that organized baseball has on the American imagination derives from the concept of loyalty to the franchise rather than to the individuals. . . . (In) the ever-changing megalopolis, loyalty to a baseball franchise offers the same assurance and stability that 'home for the holidays' does."

Tristram Potter Coffin, in The Old Ball Game

Boston fans were loyal to Manny Ramirez for nearly eight seasons, but when he outstayed his welcome and was shipped off to Los Angeles, the Red Sox Nation quickly stepped up to express their support for the newest member of the organization, Jason Bay, whom they received in exchange for Manny in 2008. In the high-stakes free-agent market that has dominated baseball for more than three decades, loyalty to individuals has become more and more difficult, but it hasn't lessened the loyalty to the Red Sox franchise of millions upon millions of fans.

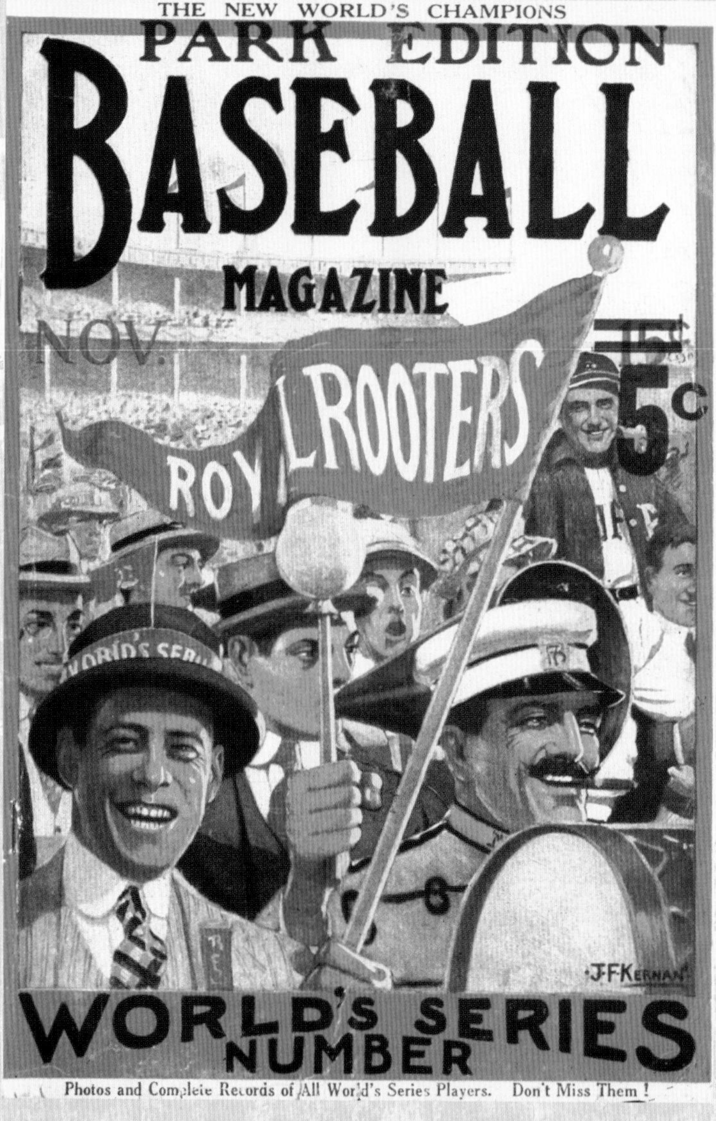

THE NEW WORLD'S CHAMPIONS

PARK EDITION

BASEBALL

MAGAZINE

NOV.

ROYAL ROOTERS

15c
5c

WORLD'S SERIES
NUMBER

J·F·KERNAN

382

Photos and Complete Records of All World's Series Players.   Don't Miss Them !

"A fanatic is one who sticks to his guns whether they're loaded or not."

Franklin P. Jones, American businessman

Although they are depicted as a rather cordial and good-natured bunch on the November 1912 edition of *Baseball Magazine*, Boston's Royal Rooters were a rough-and-tumble collection of fiercely dedicated fans who traveled far and wide to support their beloved team. During the 1903 World Series, the Rooters' boisterous presence both at home and on the road in Pittsburgh was cited by opposing players as a factor in Boston's success. While they likely didn't carry loaded guns, they were about as fanatical a group of fans as you could find.

> **"The crowd as a whole plays the role of Greek chorus to the actors on the field below. It reflects every action, every movement, every changing phase of the game. . . . The crowd lives the actions of the players more than in any other game. It is a release and something of a purge. It is the next best thing to participation."**

Paul Gallico, in Farewell to Sport

On occasion, the fans' participation in the action can go a little too far. During a game against New York in April 2005, Yankees outfielder Gary Sheffield has words with some Red Sox fans seated in the right field seats at Fenway after he accused them of interfering with his attempt to track down a hit. For the most part, though, the interaction between fans and opposing players amounts to little more than a chorus of taunts, perhaps questioning the species of a players' parents.

"The absolute fundamental aim is to make money out of satisfying customers."

Sir John Egan

This brief statement captures the essential principle that baseball business adopted long ago. The product on the field is always the foundation of this arrangement, and as a general rule, the better the team, the more money it will make. But beyond the on-field activities, myriad trinkets and accoutrements are produced to satisfy the fans' desire to express their loyalty and passion. From authentic jerseys to oversized foam fingers, avid fans are known to show up at games decked out from head to toe in Red Sox paraphernalia.

> **"In the earlier days of baseball there was a sentiment attached to the national game that made games take on the appearance of real battles between cities and section, but sentiment no longer figures in the sport. It is now only a battle of dollars."**

New York Evening Journal *editorial, October 7, 1908*

Even with the multimillion-dollar contracts and high-priced seats, the rivalry between the Red Sox and the Yankees and their host cities has remained intense for decades. Things got ugly during a game in July 2004, when a shoving match between catcher Jason Varitek and New York's Alex Rodriguez quickly escalated into a bench-clearing brawl. With the teams going head to head in the American League Championship Series in 2003 and 2004, there was always plenty at stake when the Sox and Yankees met on the diamond, even during the regular season.

"All you see in Red Sox–Yankee games are fights and cops dragging people out by the hair."

Dan Shaughnessy

Things appear to be peaceful between these fans of the heated rivals, but it's only batting practice before a game in 2006. Occasionally the passions do get out of control, and some fans have even ended up in the hospital following scuffles at Red Sox–Yankee games. The rivalry has not quite reached the fever pitch found within soccer enmities in England and other countries, but that doesn't mean the American baseball fans are any less enthusiastic about supporting their teams.

> **"Sox fans always seem to be concerned with what the Yankees are doing, and it tends to be more of a one-way obsession. I think it's true that we care more about the Yankees than they care about the Sox."**

Terry Francona

During a game at Fenway Park in June 2007, the Yankees' Alex Rodriguez was greeted by fans sporting blonde-haired masks, a response to the recent turmoil in Rodriguez's private life. Rodriguez has certainly attracted more attention from Boston fans than any Red Sox player has in New York, but he also makes the most money in baseball, so it is no wonder. With the Red Sox's success in recent years, the balance of power between the franchises has shifted, and the Sox can no longer lay claim to underdog status as easily.

"Johnny Damon looks like Jesus, acts like Judas, and throws like Mary."

Anonymous

Even a once-beloved Red Sox player such as Johnny Damon is not safe from the wrath of the Red Sox Nation, particularly after he committed the ultimate sin of signing with the Yankees. With each passing decade, the rivalry and bitterness between the New York Yankees, the Boston Red Sox, and their respective fans seems to become more intense. The competition is not simply about baseball, but about the two biggest and most powerful cities in the Northeast with millions of proud citizens.

"I think if you're Red Sox, well, it's something you're born with, an affection that you have."

Johnny Pesky

The affection of a Red Sox fan can be found in people of all ages, heights, and walks of life. It is a following that is bestowed with proverbial nation status and that reaches not just throughout Boston and Massachusetts and New England, but throughout the nation and the world. Johnny Pesky, who has worked with the Red Sox organization on and off for seven decades, understands those affections about as well as anyone.

Index

David Ortiz